BOONE COUNTY LIBRARY

2040 91 642 128 0

WITHDRAWN

D0848939

BOONE COUNTY PUBLIC LIBRARY
BURLINGTON, KY 41005
www.bcpl.org

DEC 1 6 2008

GUNSMITHING WITH SIMPLE HAND TOOLS

0   11557 00378   9

GUNSMITHING WITH SIMPLE HAND TOOLS

Andrew Dubino

Foreword by Ned Schwing

STACKPOLE
BOOKS

Copyright © 1987 by Stackpole Books

Published by
STACKPOLE BOOKS
5067 Ritter Road
Mechanicsburg, PA 17055
www.stackpolebooks.com

All rights reserved, including the right to reproduce this book or portions thereof in any form or by any means, electronic or mechanical, including photocopying, recording, or by any information storage and retrieval system, without permission in writing from the publisher. All inquiries should be addressed to Stackpole Books, 5067 Ritter Road, Mechanicsburg, PA 17055.

Printed in the United States of America

10 9 8 7 6 5 4 3 2 1

First edition

ISBN-13: 978-0-8117-0378-9
ISBN-10: 0-8117-0378-9

Library of Congress Cataloging-in-Publication Data

Dubino, Andrew
    Gunsmithing with simple hand tools.

    1. Gunsmithing – Amateurs' manuals.   I. Title
TS535.D76   1987   683.4'03   87-9960
ISBN 0-8117-0784-9

*To my wife, Nancy, for her tireless typing
and her encouragement.
To my brother, Jim, for letting me watch
while he worked.*

Contents

Foreword

In his introduction, Andrew Dubino states that he assumes his readers have a good knowledge of guns and ammo in general, but little knowledge of basic hand tools. This covers many potential readers who could benefit from this book.

Dubino takes a careful and methodical approach by first describing the basic hand tools on which he is going to focus. He then moves on to the workshop itself and details what is required to complete a successful gunsmithing project, including the myriad types of files and how to use them. About twenty-five pages are devoted to preparing and blueing a firearm. Although this particular subject requires specialized equipment, the method is explained in such a way as to be easily understood.

Dubino then discusses working with small parts such as firing pins, sight mountings, and many others. He covers side locks, lock plates, tumblers, and sears—a discussion that will be most helpful to those readers who want to work on their flint locks, percussion rifles, and shotguns. He also covers triggers, springs, and hammers, which is helpful to those who want to improve their rifle or handgun lock time. No expensive tools are needed, and the straightforward narrative enhances the reader's understanding of how these important components work together.

This book is a great resource for anyone who wants to know the inner workings of firearms and is willing to carefully follow the author's detailed instructions.

Ned Schwing

Preface

My older brother, a retired toolmaker and a gun nut with almost fifty years in the toolroom, reviewed some of the first draft work of this book. One of his comments was ". . . looks like a real basic course in toolmaking-benchwork. . . ." And why shouldn't it? What is gunsmithing but an application of the toolmaker's craft to a specific category of mechanical gadgetry. In the course of his professional life, the average gunsmith will use every tool, procedure, and shop trick that the toolmaker will employ in the toolroom. While every toolmaker is not a gunsmith, every gunsmith is a toolmaker to some degree.

This book is written for the advanced amateur who already has a good knowledge of guns and ammo in general. The concentration is on the use of basic hand tools and hand metal-removal tools and their application in the fabrication of small parts for the gun. Although it assumes he or she already has a good knowledge of guns, it assumes the opposite with regard to the tools and procedures covered. No doubt the professional gunsmith would find its contents basic and the total coverage incomplete. But then, it isn't written to the level of the professional; it is written for the amateur who has a desire to "dress up" or execute minor alterations to his favorite shooter, or perhaps put a valued but not too valuable heirloom in working condition.

No reference is made to ballistics, reloading, action types and operations, trouble shooting, and performance theory in general. There are already numerous superb books on all of these subjects, ranging in depth from the beginner's introduction to the highly technical. It would be redundant to attempt coverage of these areas here. Nor does this book touch on those facets of gunsmithing where safety could be jeopardized if the work were improperly done, such as re-barreling or chambering. That work is better left to the professional with the proper equipment.

Acknowledgments

Appreciation is extended to the following firms for supplying materials and information used in writing this book:

Brownells, Inc.   Montezuma, Iowa
Grobet File Co.   Carlstadt, New Jersey
Nicholson File Co.   Apex, North Carolina
Simonds Cutting Tools   Fitchburg, Massachusetts
Starrett Co.   Athol, Massachusetts
W. T. McBride, Inc.   West Springfield, Massachusetts

Also to George Katsar, master rodmaker and photographer, and to Lynn Kline for her isometric drawings.

1

An Argument
in Favor

How often has the average shooter had an overwhelming desire to convert his almost-perfect pet firearm into the perfect piece? Perhaps a milled, all-steel trigger guard to replace the stamped guard would do the trick. Maybe he needs a complex spring for that magnificent antique that has been gathering dust in the attic. One day he'll descend upon his local gunsmith or machine shop, finally determined to have the work done. Often as not, he'll stagger away in a daze when he discovers the cost.

The gunsmith and machinist are not rip-off artists. What might seem a simple operation to the layman usually involves a large number of machine tool setups, special tooling, and time for the professional. Remember, those poor guys are in business to make a living. Every time the clock ticks, they must take in a certain amount of money, or they won't be in business long. The pet project is simply not cost-effective if someone else is to do the work.

The average consumer of today too often assumes that everything must be made by machine tools. Let's take a brief look at the history of machine tool development just to prove one point: how short a period of time the machine tool has occupied in history.

The first screw-cutting lathe with a leadscrew and change gears is generally considered to be the development of Henry Maudslay, an Englishman, in 1797. Shortly thereafter, one of his lathes found its way to America, in violation of an English law that prohibited the export of machinery. Capitalizing on Maudslay's lathe, American mechanics improved on the basic design. In 1853 George Freeland produced an all-iron lathe, the forerunner of today's engine lathe.

The metal-cutting shaper was developed in 1836 by James Nasmyth, another Englishman. Eli Whitney is credited with the development of the plain milling machine in about 1818. About 1861, Joseph Brown invented the first universal milling machine. Advertisements began appearing in trade journals for a surface grinder around 1876.

The advent of the Civil War made such demands on American industry that American machine tool development began to lead the world. And yet, even with all these revolutionary developments in machine tool technology, the surface grinder did not find general acceptance in the machine shop until the late 1880s. The final precision fitting and finishing of surfaces was done with the hand file. Until two hundred years ago, almost everything was handmade.

Too often we tend to associate quality of workmanship with modern machine tool production. The term *handmade* has gradually become synonymous with *crude*. We go to the local craft fairs and expect to see handmade products. We're seldom disappointed because many of them certainly fit our image of handmade. But occasionally we encounter real craftsmen whose products far surpass anything that could be turned out on a machine in workmanship, design, and detail. If you have any doubts about the quality of work that can be produced with hand tools, look carefully at a fine set of eighteenth-century English or French dueling pistols. Then consider that the lathe, shaper, milling machine, and surface grinder had not yet been invented.

Many freely acknowledge the artistry of a true craftsman. They tend, however, to ascribe almost supernatural talents to such a person. He is one in a million, they say, a man born to the craft. How often have we heard, "They just don't make craftsmen like they used to?" Certainly, the average individual of today is better educated, better informed, and healthier, and most likely has better eyesight and physical dexterity than his counterpart of two or three hundred years ago. Nowhere in my readings have I discovered that the cabinetmaker, gunsmith, or any other old-time craftsman was specially selected by a battery of psychological tests to determine his suitability for a trade. These craftsmen certainly must have been numerous, because they produced almost all of the consumer goods then available.

Most often they were self-taught or, if lucky, apprenticed to a master. They worked at their trade because there was a demand for their services. Their motivation for excellence was prompted by competition for their job from other craftsmen within the trade, just like today. I doubt that they were any more enthralled with their jobs than the average workers of today, and they would most likely have chosen to work at something that paid better and required shorter hours.

Today's shortage of real craftsmen has created such an aura of mystique about the individual who can produce with his hands that anyone with a secret desire to do the same thing is frightened away. We still have a number of superior artisans making a living at their craft. But the number is small because the demand for their services is limited. Those who are superior and well known command prices that only the wealthy can afford. The competition today for the individual proficient with his hands is the machine tool, mass production, and time.

I began my gunsmithing career at 13, specifically, the day my older brother left for the army in World War II. It was only then that I could go into his workshop and use his tools without receiving a belt on the ear. Until then, I could only watch him work. His tools consisted of some old, worn-out, and discarded files, saws, and taps and dies, along with other miscellaneous junk. It wasn't too long before I was able to make a usable firing pin or extractor. I even made a crude action to attach to an old .22 long rifle barrel with these tools. Throughout the years, I worked in several gunshops around the country where the file and hacksaw were the major, if not the only, tools. It wasn't until many years later that I could afford a modern toolroom setup of my own, with all the ancillary tooling. Even then, I found myself spending almost half my time at the bench with either a file or a hacksaw in my hand. With about $75,000 worth of machinery and tooling at hand, I often lacked the special cutter or fixture necessary to make one small, complex part. The most practical way to do the job was with a file and hacksaw.

Used in the proper combinations, the file, hacksaw, drill, hammer, and chisel can, within reason, duplicate the functions of most machine tools. The main difference is that the machine tool, when properly tooled and set up, does the work in a small fraction of the time needed for hand tools and usually requires an operator with much less skill than is necessary for precision handwork. But, whereas time is money to the man in business, the hobbiest can afford as much time as he needs for his project. The principles underlying the use of hand tools are few and simple. Almost anyone can be taught rather quickly to produce functional gadgets with this type of tool. However, the file, hacksaw, and drill can also produce superb finished products. The difference between the "mowing machine mechanic" and the craftsman is the craftsman's meticulous attention to detail and desire for excellence.

A tremendous quantity and variety of quality hand tools are readily available in today's market. The craftsman of two or three hundred years ago would be astonished if he were to walk into an average hardware store today. Many hand tools are already present in the basement or garage workshop. From time to time I go through the kitchen drawers to find the tools that my wife squirrels away for her household needs. My efforts are usually rewarded with tools that meet about 25 percent of my workshop needs.

Almost anyone with the physical and mental attributes necessary to read a newspaper, tie a shoe, walk across the street, or discharge a firearm already possesses the qualities necessary to be a skilled craftsman. A little effort and time will prove that. It is only necessary to "unpsych" oneself from the erroneous notion that the skilled artisan is a born superman with talents and powers beyond the average mortal's reach.

2

Basic Hand Tools

For the purposes of this book, basic hand tools will be divided into five categories: layout and marking tools, holding tools, measuring tools, cutting tools, and some miscellaneous equipment.

Many of the tools to be described can be used for working with either wood or metal. It is always the better practice, however, to use the tool only on the material for which it was designed. This is especially true of holding and cutting tools. What usually differentiates a wood-working from a metal-working tool is that the latter is more accurately made, and in the case of cutting tools, of a harder and tougher steel, with different cutting angles.

Within each category listed above there are many varieties, sizes, and configurations. To describe each in detail is beyond the scope of this book. Only a few from each category will be described. An examination of manufacturers' catalogs will give some idea of just how much is available. Additionally, these catalogs are an excellent source of specialized technical information. Many readers are already familiar with some of these tools and how to manipulate them. Their use will be described here in general terms only. Specific usage will be covered in later chapters, as it applies to the project being covered.

LAYOUT AND MARKING TOOLS

Any project worthy of the effort must proceed in an orderly, disciplined sequence. It is not enough to get an idea and then attack the project material, removing chunks that don't fit a mental picture. Even something as simple as sawing a piece off a board requires a layout if it is to be done properly. This is usually a line scribed with a pencil. In this case the pencil is the marking tool, and a straightedge is the layout tool. More elaborate patterns would probably require development and refinement on paper and transferral to the material being worked. In this case more layout equipment would be required. Layout and marking tools are lumped into one category because some perform both functions simultaneously.

The French curve, straightedge, protractor, and square are pure layout tools (figure 1). They serve only as guides to a marking instrument for scribing a predetermined line. The French curve can provide

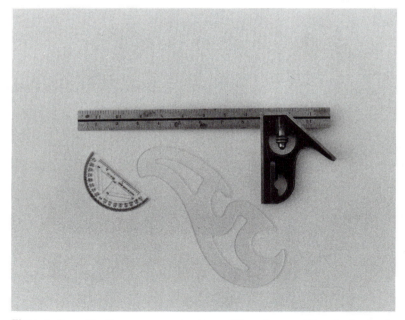

Figure 1. A combination square, protractor, and French curve. These basic, simple layout tools, already found in most home workshops, will adequately serve for almost any layout job that the home craftsman may encounter.

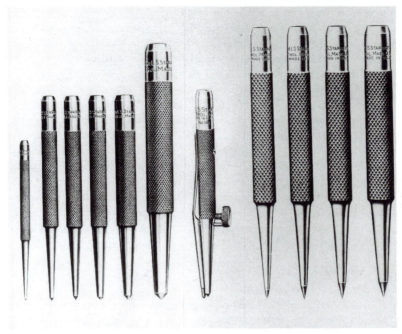

Figure 2. An assortment of prick punches and center punches. The seventh punch from the right is a spacing center punch. It can be set in a manner similar to a compass or divider and used to make a series of similarly spaced punches. Great for layout work. (Courtesy of L.S. Starrett Co.)

a guide for a line of practically any degree of simple or compound curvature. The straightedge and square are obviously intended as guides for straight lines. The square also serves to determine right angles. A compass can be classified as both a marking and a layout tool. It is used primarily on material that can be marked with pencil or ink. To scribe a circle on metal, a set of dividers is used. A quick-drying, dark blue or red fluid is usually painted or sprayed on metal before scribing. This is called layout fluid. Its purpose is to highlight the scribed line.

Scribes and punches are strictly marking tools. Figure 2 illustrates two types of punch, prink punches and center punches. A prick punch is much more slender and makes a smaller indentation in the metal to be marked. This slender configuration and small indentation permit greater accuracy in locating the initial mark. A center punch is then used to deepen and widen the mark. The spacing center punch is a handy variation of the standard center punch. Equally spaced punch marks can be made accurately simply by setting the guide point to the required spacing, as one would set a compass or dividers.

HOLDING TOOLS

This category covers a multitude of general and specialized tools. There are fixtures for holding complex shapes; pneumatically operated clamping tools and chucks; precision toolmakers' vises, accurate to 0.0005 inch; and special vises and collets for a variety of machine tools. We'll concern ourselves with only two: the bench vise and toolmakers' parallel clamps (figure 3). It's fairly safe to say that 99 percent of all benchwork can be done with these two tools to hold the workpiece. A good quality machinists' vise with 4-inch jaws and a pair of 3-inch toolmakers' clamps will serve most needs.

MEASURING TOOLS

Almost every machinist's toolbox will contain a 1-inch micrometer, a 6-inch dial or vernier caliper, and a 6-inch steel rule (figure 4). These are the three basic measuring tools. The micrometer, available with either 0.001 or 0.0001 graduations, is capable of measuring to that accuracy when the proper touch is developed. The dial or vernier caliper is graduated in 0.001 inches. Generally, a slightly more accurate measurement can be obtained with the average micrometer, but the caliper has the advantages of being quicker and being capable of measuring out to 6 inches and usually has provisions for measuring depths to 6 inches. Its accuracy is sufficient for most benchwork. The rule is graduated in $\frac{1}{8}$, $\frac{1}{16}$, $\frac{1}{32}$, and $\frac{1}{64}$ inches.

CUTTING TOOLS

These are the tools that give shape and dimension to the material being worked. Generally, wood-cutting tools are made of a fairly high carbon steel called carbon tool steel. When properly heat-treated, this steel is capable of attaining a high degree of hardness and a keen cutting edge. Many metal-cutting tools are still made with carbon steel. However, carbon steel does not provide very good wear resistance when used on metal, and when heated by the friction caused by cutting, it will lose its hardness.

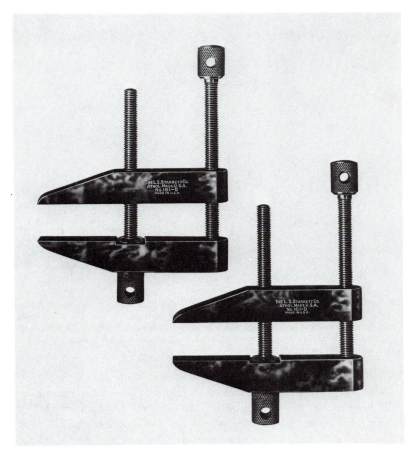

Figure 3. Toolmakers' clamps. Although the standard **C** clamp has its uses in the machine shop, the above clamps are much more versatile in metal work. They are, in fact, a portable vise. The long, slender jaws enable them to be used in clamping situations impossible for a **C** clamp. (Courtesy of L.S. Starrett Co.)

The addition of tungsten, chromium, and vanadium to a high carbon steel produces an improved cutting steel commonly called high-speed tool steel. Although it is not harder than carbon tool steel, it has much greater wear resistance and maintains its cutting edge even at temperatures that turn it a dull red. Many sophisticated materials for cutting metal are now available: carbide, ceramics, dia-

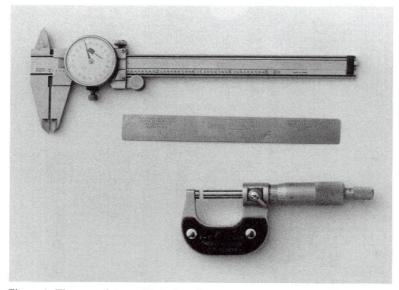

Figure 4. There are few machinists' toolboxes that don't contain a 6-inch dial or vernier caliper, 6-inch rule, and a 1-inch micrometer. If you can afford all three, buy them. If you can only afford one, opt for the 6-inch dial caliper. It will enable you to take measurements for outside and inside and depth to an accuracy of plus or minus 0.001 inch.

monds, and artificial substances with the hardness of a diamond. Yet the high-speed steel cutting tool is the most common cutting tool in most machine shops. Slightly more expensive than a comparable carbon steel tool, it is well worth the additional cost and highly recommended as the tool to choose when there is a choice.

The saw, twist drill, reamer, and file are the cutting tools that will concern us. Within reason and size limitations, these tools, used in combination, can duplicate many machine tool functions with amazing accuracy. It's a rare home garage or basement that can't produce an electric hand drill with a plastic case of six of the most-used twist drills for home repair. The hacksaw and an 8- or 10-inch file can usually be found in most home work areas. The variety of sizes, shapes, configurations, and special applications for twist drills, reamers, and files is so extensive that even most machine shops do not stock the full lines. The file, in particular, is available in so many sizes, shapes, and cuts and has such a wide variety of uses that a future chapter will be devoted entirely to it.

Twist drills come in fractional sizes, letter sizes, and number sizes. Fractional sizes usually start at ¹⁄₁₆ inch and proceed to 1¼ inch by ¹⁄₆₄-inch increments. Beyond 1¼ inches they generally increase in size by ¹⁄₃₂-inch increments. Number size drills begin at No. 80 (0.0135 inch) and proceed to No. 1 (0.228 inch) in increments that mesh with, but do not duplicate, fractional sizes within that range. Letter sizes start with A (0.234 inch) and proceed to Z (0.413 inch). They take over where the number sizes leave off and mesh with fractional sizes in the same manner. Table 1 gives a consecutive listing of drill sizes in fractional, number, letter, and metric, and their equivalent decimal size up to 1 inch.

The most common twist drill, the general purpose, functions adequately in most materials. This is usually the only drill found in local hardware stores that is suitable for metal. For the more specialized drills, go to an industrial supply house. These specialized drills are the fast spiral for use in aluminum and soft materials and the slow special for use in brass and plastics, deep-hole worm patterns, and a large variety of lengths and shank configurations.

The twist drill cannot be considered a precision metal removal tool. Various engineering reference manuals give it an accuracy tolerance up to +0.005 inch. This tolerance assumes using either a new drill or one sharpened by a machine. A drill sharpened freehand on a grinder can almost always be counted on to drill beyond this tolerance and larger than the drill diameter, commensurate with the skill of the individual doing the sharpening. Additionally, a twist drill will not produce a perfectly round hole, and the finish will be quite rough. In spite of its shortcomings, it still produces results adequate for most purposes and can be considered one of the most useful of metal-removal tools.

When a more accurate hole is needed, a drilled hole is enlarged with a reamer to the exact desired size. The reamer can produce a hole accurate to within +0.0001 to +0.0005 inch, with a good internal finish and near-perfect roundness. Standard size reamers come in the same sizes as twist drills; fractional, number, and letter. The most commonly used reamers are those used to produce a straight hole of uniform diameter. There are, however, reamers to produce a variety of internal configurations, ranging from a simple straight taper to a

Table 1 — Drill Sizes and Their Decimal Equivalents

Size	Decimal Equivalents	Size	Decimal Equivalents
No. 80	0.0135		
No. 79	0.0145	No. 55	0.0520
1/64	0.0156	1.35mm	0.0531
No. 78	0.0160	No. 54	0.0550
No. 77	0.0180	1.40mm	0.0551
.5mm	0.0197	1.45mm	0.0571
No. 76	0.0200	1.50mm	0.0590
No. 75	0.0210	No. 53	0.0595
No. 74	0.0225	1.55mm	0.0610
.6mm	0.0236	1/16	0.0625
No. 73	0.0240	1.60mm	0.0630
No. 72	0.0250	No. 52	0.0635
No. 71	0.0260	1.65mm	0.0649
.7mm	0.0276	1.70mm	0.0669
No. 70	0.0280	No. 51	0.0670
No. 69	0.0292	1.75mm	0.0689
.75mm	0.0295	No. 50	0.0700
No. 68	0.0310	1.80mm	0.0708
1/32	0.0312	1.85mm	0.0728
.8mm	0.0315	No. 49	0.0730
No. 67	0.0320	1.90mm	0.0748
No. 66	0.0330	No. 48	0.0760
No. 65	0.0350	1.95mm	0.0767
.9mm	0.0354	5/64	0.0781
No. 64	0.0360	No. 47	0.0785
No. 63	0.0370	2.00mm	0.0787
No. 62	0.0380	2.05mm	0.0807
No. 61	0.0390	No. 46	0.0810
1.00mm	0.0393	No. 45	0.0820
No. 60	0.0400	2.10mm	0.0827
No. 59	0.0410	2.15mm	0.0846
1.05mm	0.0413	No. 44	0.0860
No. 58	0.0420	2.20mm	0.0866
No. 57	0.0430	2.25mm	0.0886
1.10mm	0.0433	No. 43	0.0890
1.15mm	0.0452	2.30mm	0.0906
No. 56	0.0465	2.35mm	0.0925
3/64	0.0469	No. 42	0.0935
1.20mm	0.0472	3/32	0.0937
1.25mm	0.0492	2.40mm	0.0945
1.30mm	0.0511	No. 41	0.0960

Table 1 — continued

Size	Decimal Equivalents	Size	Decimal Equivalents
2.45mm	0.0965	No. 22	0.1570
No. 40	0.0980	4.00mm	0.1574
2.50mm	0.0984	No. 21	0.1590
No. 39	0.0995	No. 20	0.1610
No. 38	0.1015	4.10mm	0.1614
2.60mm	0.1024	4.20mm	0.1653
No. 37	0.1040	No. 19	0.1660
2.70mm	0.1063	4.25mm	0.1673
No. 36	0.1065	4.30mm	0.1692
2.75mm	0.1083	No. 18	0.1695
7/64	0.1094	11/64	0.1719
No. 35	0.1100	No. 17	0.1730
2.80mm	0.1102	4.40mm	0.1732
No. 34	0.1110	No. 16	0.1770
No. 33	0.1130	4.50mm	0.1771
2.90mm	0.1142	No. 15	0.1800
No. 32	0.1160	4.60mm	0.1811
3.00mm	0.1181	No. 14	0.1820
No. 31	0.1200	No. 13	0.1850
3.10mm	0.1220	4.70mm	0.1850
1/8	0.1250	4.75mm	0.1870
3.20mm	0.1260	3/16	0.1875
3.25mm	0.1279	4.80mm	0.1889
No. 30	0.1285	No. 12	0.1890
3.30mm	0.1299	No. 11	0.1910
3.40mm	0.1339	4.90mm	0.1929
No. 29	0.1360	No. 10	0.1935
3.50mm	0.1378	No. 9	0.1960
No. 28	0.1405	5.00mm	0.1968
9/64	0.1406	No. 8	0.1990
3.60mm	0.1417	5.10mm	0.2007
No. 27	0.1440	No. 7	0.2010
3.70mm	0.1457	13/64	0.2031
No. 26	0.1470	No. 6	0.2040
3.75mm	0.1476	5.20mm	0.2047
No. 25	0.1495	No. 5	0.2055
3.80mm	0.1496	5.25mm	0.2067
No. 24	0.1520	5.30mm	0.2087
3.90mm	0.1535	No. 4	0.2090
No. 23	0.1540	5.40mm	0.2126
5/32	0.1562	No. 3	0.2130

Table 1 — continued

Size	Decimal Equivalents	Size	Decimal Equivalents
5.50mm	0.2165	L	0.2900
7/32	0.2187	7.40mm	0.2913
5.60mm	0.2205	M	0.2950
No. 2	0.2210	7.50mm	0.2952
5.70mm	0.2244	19/64	0.2969
5.75mm	0.2264	7.60mm	0.2992
No. 1	0.2280	N	0.3020
5.80mm	0.2283	7.70mm	0.3031
5.90mm	0.2323	7.75mm	0.3051
A	0.2340	7.80mm	0.3071
15/64	0.2344	7.90mm	0.3110
6.00mm	0.2362	5/16	0.3125
B	0.2380	8.00mm	0.3149
6.10mm	0.2402	O	0.3160
C	0.2420	8.10mm	0.3189
6.20mm	0.2441	8.20mm	0.3228
D	0.2460	P	0.3230
6.25mm	0.2461	8.25mm	0.3248
6.30mm	0.2480	8.30mm	0.3267
1/4	0.2500	21/64	0.3281
E	0.2500	8.40mm	0.3307
6.40mm	0.2520	Q	0.3320
6.50mm	0.2559	8.50mm	0.3346
F	0.2570	8.60mm	0.3385
6.60mm	0.2598	R	0.3390
G	0.2610	8.70mm	0.3425
6.70mm	0.2638	11/32	0.3437
17/64	0.2656	8.75mm	0.3444
6.75mm	0.2657	8.80mm	0.3464
H	0.2660	S	0.3480
6.80mm	0.2677	8.90mm	0.3503
6.90mm	0.2717	9.00mm	0.3543
I	0.2720	T	0.3580
7.00mm	0.2756	9.10mm	0.3583
J	0.2770	23/64	0.3594
7.10mm	0.2795	9.20mm	0.3622
K	0.2810	9.25mm	0.3642
9/32	0.2812	9.30mm	0.3661
7.20mm	0.2834	U	0.3680
7.25mm	0.2854	9.40mm	0.3701
7.30mm	0.2874	9.50mm	0.3740

Table 1 – continued

Size	Decimal Equivalents	Size	Decimal Equivalents
3/8	0.3750	16.5mm	0.6496
V	0.3770	21/32	0.6562
9.60mm	0.3780	17.0mm	0.6693
9.70mm	0.3819	43/64	0.6719
9.75mm	0.3839	11/16	0.6875
9.80mm	0.3858	17.5mm	0.6890
W	0.3860	45/64	0.7031
9.90mm	0.3898	18.0mm	0.7087
25/64	0.3906	23/32	0.7187
10.00mm	0.3937	18.5mm	0.7283
X	0.3970	47/64	0.7344
Y	0.4040	19.0mm	0.7480
13/32	0.4062	3/4	0.7500
Z	0.4130	49/64	0.7656
10.50mm	0.4134	19.5mm	0.7677
27/64	0.4219	25/32	0.7812
11.00mm	0.4331	20.0mm	0.7874
7/16	0.4375	51/64	0.7969
11.50mm	0.4528	20.5mm	0.8071
29/64	0.4531	13/16	0.8125
15/32	0.4687	21.0mm	0.8268
12.00mm	0.4724	53/64	0.8281
31/64	0.4844	27/32	0.8437
12.50mm	0.4921	21.5mm	0.8465
1/2	0.5000	55/64	0.8594
13.0mm	0.5118	22.0mm	0.8661
33/64	0.5156	7/8	0.8750
17/32	0.5313	22.5mm	0.8858
13.5mm	0.5315	57/64	0.8906
35/64	0.5469	23.0mm	0.9055
14.0mm	0.5512	29/32	0.9062
9/16	0.5625	59/64	0.9219
14.5mm	0.5709	23.5mm	0.9252
37/64	0.5781	15/16	0.9375
15.0mm	0.5906	24.0mm	0.9449
19/32	0.5937	61/64	0.9531
39/64	0.6094	24.5mm	0.9646
15.5mm	0.6102	31/32	0.9687
5/8	0.6250	25.0mm	0.9843
16.0mm	0.6299	63/64	0.9844
41/64	0.6406	1	1.0000

Courtesy of W. T. McBride Co., Inc.

combination of tapers, straight holes, and shoulders. The chambers in rifle and shotgun barrels are cut with reamers. These reamers are usually called forming reamers and are highly specialized tools.

As with twist drills, reamers come in several varieties of shank and flute configurations. There are taper shank reamers, chucking reamers with straight shanks, and straight shank reamers with squares milled on the end of the shanks (figure 5). The latter are called hand reamers because the reamer is held in a suitable wrench by the square end and is powered by hand. Taper shank and chucking reamers are for machine use. The various flute configurations are the straight flute, spiral flute, and helical flute. The spiral and helical flute reamers provide a shearing cut, which will give a slightly smoother finish and is particularly helpful when reaming holes with keyways and grooves. The spiral will bridge the keyway or groove, thus preventing chatter

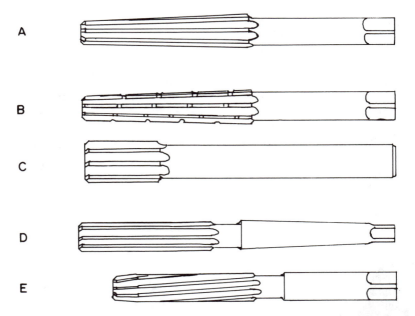

Figure 5. An assortment of reamers: *A*, Finish taper hand reamer. *B*, Rough taper hand reamer. *C*, Straight flute chucking reamer for machine use. *D*, Straight flute taper shank reamer for machine use. *E*, Left-hand spiral hand reamer. Note that all hand reamers have squares milled on the end of the shank.

**Table 2 — Teeth Selector Chart and Recommended
Saw Speeds for Hand Hacksaws**

Material	Teeth per Inch	Strokes per Minute
Ferrous		
BX	32	60
Conduit, rigid	24	60
Drill rod	18–24	40
Iron, cast	14	60
Pipe	18–24	60
Rails	14	40
Sheet metal	24–32	60
Steel, machinery	14–18	60
Steel, tool	18–24	50
Structural shapes, heavy	14–18	60
Structural shapes, light	18–24	60
Tubing, light	24–32	60
Nonferrous		
Aluminum	14	60
Brass and bronze	14–24	60
Brass tubing	24	60
Copper	14	60
Structural shapes	14–24	60
Nonmetal		
Asbestos	14	60
Fiber	14	60
Slate	14	60

and eliminating the possibility that the flute will dig into the groove
(a common occurrence with a straight flute reamer).

The hand hacksaw is probably the most universal of all hand saws.
It will cut materials ranging from plastics, wood, and nonferrous
metal to unhardened carbon and alloy steels. The blades are dispos-
able, relatively inexpensive, and available in most hardware stores. In
short, no home should be without one.

Hacksaw blades are made in 10- and 12-inch lengths and are ½
inch wide and .025 inch thick. Tooth selection is generally 14, 18, 24,
and 32 teeth per inch. The teeth selector chart (table 2) gives the

recommended teeth per inch for sawing various materials. It should be noted that the thinner the material being cut (i.e., tubing, conduit, sheet metal), the more teeth per inch are recommended. The reason is that the more teeth in contact with the material, the less chance that the teeth will snag on the edges. Conversely, even a coarse blade with 14 or 18 teeth per inch will usually have sufficient teeth in contact with a thick piece of material. The larger and coarser teeth will remove more material per stroke, thus providing a faster cut.

MISCELLANEOUS

Several tools in this category could also be listed in the groups above. The tap and die, for instance, are cutting tools in a sense. They both remove metal in a cutting action. However, their use is limited to a specific function, under specific conditions — the production of threads in relatively exact inside diameter or on an outside diameter of similar exactness. As with most other tools, there are many variations in tap and die configurations, thread type, method of use, and so on. The hand tap and the round split die are the ones most likely to be used by the gunsmith.

The tap we will concern ourselves with is the straight flute made with two, three, or four flutes. The threaded portion is approximately the same length as the shank, with a square milled on the end of the shank. This square fits into a tap wrench. In years long gone by, every maker of mechanical gadgetry had his own thread specifications; now, all threads are standardized. The Unified Thread Form and the American National Standard Thread are the basis of this standardization, specifying substantially the same thread form so that parts are mechanically interchangeable. The principal difference is the variation of tolerance with size. Unified threads are designated UNC (Unified Coarse) or UNF (Unified Fine), with the thread size following: i.e., UNC 10-24, UNF 10-32.

American National threads are designated NC (National Coarse), or NF (National Fine) with the thread size following: i.e., NC 10-24, NF 10-32. The first number designates the largest physical diameter of the screw thread (major diameter) and the second number, the threads per inch. Thread sizes are designated by either screw number size (0, 1, 2, 3, 4, 5, 6, 8, 10, 12) or fractional size in $\frac{1}{16}$-inch increments. (Screw number sizes do not correspond to drill number sizes.) The fractional designation usually begins with $\frac{1}{4}$ inch. Table 3

TABLE 3
Tap Drill and Body Drill Sizes

Thread Size	Tap Drill	Body Hole, Close Fit	Body Hole, Loose Fit
0–80	56	52	50
1–72	53	48	46
1–64	53	48	46
2–64	50	43	41
2–56	50	43	41
3–56	45	37	35
3–48	47	37	35
4–48	42	32	30
4–40	43	32	30
4–36	44	32	30
5–44	37	30	29
5–40	38	30	29
6–48	31	26	25
6–40	33	26	25
6–36	34	26	25
6–32	36	26	25
8–40	28	18	16
8–36	29	18	16
8–32	29	18	16
10–32	21	9	8
10–24	25	9	8
12–28	14	2	I
12–24	16	2	I
$1/4$–28	3	F	H
$1/4$–24	4	F	H
$1/4$–20	7	F	H
$5/16$–24	I	P	Q
$5/16$–18	F	P	Q
$3/8$–24	Q	W	X
$3/8$–16	$5/16$	W	X
$7/16$–20	$25/64$	$29/64$	$15/32$
$7/16$–14	U	$29/64$	$15/32$
$1/2$–20	$29/64$	$33/64$	$17/32$
$1/2$–13	$27/64$	$33/64$	$17/32$

Courtesy of Simonds Cutting Tools.

gives a consecutive listing of tap sizes with corresponding thread availability.

Tap drill charts are available that give the proper size drill to use with a particular size and threads per inch tap. These are fine, but not always at fingertip. On occasion, a special tap with threads per inch may be used that does not appear on any chart. A simple and quick way to determine the drill size utilizes the following formula:

$$\text{Tap drill size} = \text{major diameter} - \frac{1}{\text{number of threads per inch}}$$

Example: $\frac{1}{4} - 20$ tap

Tap drill size $= 0.250 - \frac{1}{20} = 0.250 - 0.050 = 0.200$

Table 1 indicates that the No. 7 drill (0.201) is the closest and next larger drill to 0.200. This, then, is the drill to use. Always use the next larger size if the exact size isn't available. Drill sizes in decimal size are usually indicated on most drill indexes.

The round split die that is most used in gunsmithing usually has a outside diameter of $\frac{13}{16}$ inch or 1 inch. The purpose of the split is to allow slight adjustments in the final diameter of the thread to be cut. The adjustment can be made by a fine thread screw that forces the die to open as the screw is moved forward. When retracted, the spring action of the die causes it to close. The die stock will hold any adjustment in rigid position. Dies are designated in the same way as taps for thread size purposes.

3

The Workshop

These are the most important requirements of any work area:
- Sufficient space to accommodate all of the equipment to be used and still permit work room.
- Sufficient lighting to see what you're doing.
- A comfortable, dry atmosphere.

To assign arbitrary specific dimensions and specifications to the above requirements would be unrealistic. That space that is available to the home craftsman is the space that will be used, and everything else will be tailored to fit. Lighting and climatic comfort, however, are variables that can be improved. Personally, I like fluorescent lighting. Figure 6 shows a corner of my present work area. Three double 8-foot fluorescent fixtures provide sufficient light for bench work, the lathe, and a drill press behind the lathe. If the bench were the only thing that would require illumination, a pair of double 4-foot fixtures directly over the bench would be sufficient. Most home workshops are in the basement. If this is the case, ample heat is available in the wintertime to provide reasonable working comfort. In the spring and summer, unfortunately, most basements are damp. A dehumidifier of adequate

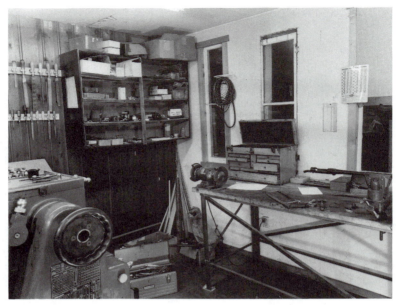

Figure 6. A corner of the author's work area. It would be more practical if the bench were up against the left wall, where the files are hanging from wall clips. However, space and other factors precluded this luxury.

capacity becomes a necessity not only for personal comfort but also to keep tools from rusting.

Adequate shelf space should be constructed for those items that can be stored on a shelf. Certain tools, such as general-purpose screwdrivers, files, pliers, and chisels, should be kept in wall-mounted clips. This is especially true of files, which become damaged easily from banging against each other. These clips are inexpensive and available in most hardware stores. As can be seen from figure 6, mine are mounted away from the bench. If I had my druthers, they would be mounted directly over the bench. Unfortunately, the window behind the bench would not permit this.

BENCH SETUP

It is almost impossible to assign priority to the various tools in a workshop. As far as I'm concerned, they're all of equal importance. This is also true of the work bench, which should be considered a tool.

In a professional machine shop, the benches are solid, level, and almost always the same height. They are designed so that the person using them does his work standing up. Conversely, the bench in the average home workshop may range anywhere from a discarded card table to a rickety contraption constructed of odds-and-ends boards and some ¼-inch plywood. You cannot do your best work on such a setup. Figure 7 shows plans for a serviceable bench that can be constructed at a reasonable cost. Your local lumber company should be able to cut the 1½-inch subflooring used for the top to required dimensions. The length and width in the drawing are ideal for most work but are certainly not sacred. Adapt the dimensions to your available space. However, adhere to the height. For the average person, this is the ideal work height. The 1½-inch sections of 2-inch

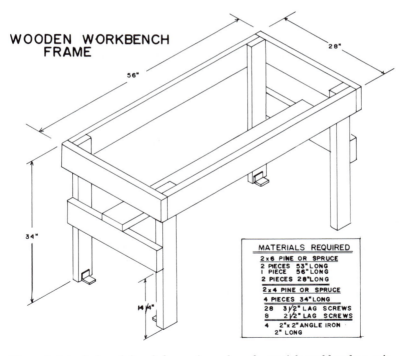

Figure 7. A typical work bench frame. A number of materials could make a suitable top. One suggestion is to use 1½-inch plywood subflooring, which your local lumber company can cut to size.

angle iron bolted to the bottom of the legs are used to bolt the bench legs to the floor. If at all possible, the back of the bench should be secured to a solid wall. In short, the setup should be solid as a rock.

TOOLS

Perhaps 50 percent of the hand tools used by the average gunsmith can be purchased at the local supermarket, drugstore, or variety store. They are usually inexpensive, attractive, and not worth a damn. The same kinds of tools purchased from a reputable industrial supplier might cost considerably more, but you can count on them doing the job properly and giving good service. When working on a limited budget, purchase for quality, rather than quantity. You can usually manage to do with fewer tools of quality. With junk tools, you may be working with less than nothing. A lot of junk is imported from such places as Taiwan, Hong Kong, Poland, and China. This is the stuff that usually winds up in the supermarkets. However, don't totally overlook imports. They also produce quality tools at reasonable prices. If you should find them in the catalog of a reputable industrial supplier, you can assume with reasonable safety that they are quality tools.

THE VISE

A most important tool — don't compromise on this one. At a minimum, the vise should have a 3½-inch jaw width and a 4-inch opening and be heavily constructed. If you can afford it, get a bigger one. Desirable additional features include a swivel base and swivel jaws. Almost all vises have replaceable jaws, and most are serrated. A set of smooth jaws is highly desirable for many kinds of work. If you can get a set with the vise, do so. If you can't buy a set, it's quite simple to make one from flat cold roll stock. Simply get a length of cold roll steel the same thickness and width as the existing jaw, cut to length, and drill the screw holes in the same place as on the existing jaws. Padding for the jaws is easily made from sheet lead or sheet brass. Cut two sheets the same length as the jaws and about 2 inches wide. Clamp both sheets in the vise and bend each sheet over its respective jaw. With a hammer, pound the bends so that the juncture is sharp and even and the overlap conforms to the rest of the vise. Padding is highly desirable to prevent marring delicate work.

Figure 6 shows my vise mounted on the right-hand side of the bench. When I tried to come up with a reason for this position, I couldn't. It's simply a matter of "that's the way I always did it." Whichever end of the bench suits you is the better end on which to put it. Just be sure the vise is mounted close enough to the front edge of the bench to permit clamping a long piece of work so that it will clear the bench top.

SCREWDRIVERS

We have all seen some otherwise fine old rifles and shotguns with chewed-up screw slots, damaged screw heads, and the area around a screw badly marred. The explanation is simple. Someone used an improperly shaped or wrong size screwdriver for the job. Figure 8 illustrates right and wrong screwdriver shapes. Note that in *A* the sides of the screwdriver are parallel to the screw slot sides. This permits the full torque from the screwdriver to be evenly transmitted to the sides of the slot in the direction of rotation. *B*, on the other hand, is a wedge-shaped screwdriver in a parallel slot. Contact is made only on the top edges of the slot. This is the only area that receives the full impact of the torque. Additionally, an upward camming action is initiated between the parallel screw slot and the wedge-shape driver whenever torque is applied, causing the screwdriver to jump out of the slot. The combination of these two undesirable features will result in a chewed-up slot and possible marring of surrounding area.

I seldom push a particular brand of product unless I think it is so good that it deserves all the recognition it can get. Figure 9 is a set of interchangeable tips that are magnetically held on the screwdriver shank. There is a tip width and thickness for just about any screw slot size encountered in gun work, and they are properly shaped. Without question, this is the finest set of screwdrivers I've used for gun work.

TWIST DRILLS

You can easily spend $200-plus on a drill set and index that will include all of the number, letter, and fractional sizes up to ½ inch. If you have the money to spend, fine. There's no doubt that sometime in your lifetime you'll use every one of the drills. However, most people don't have that kind of money, so we'll tailor our drill selection to the

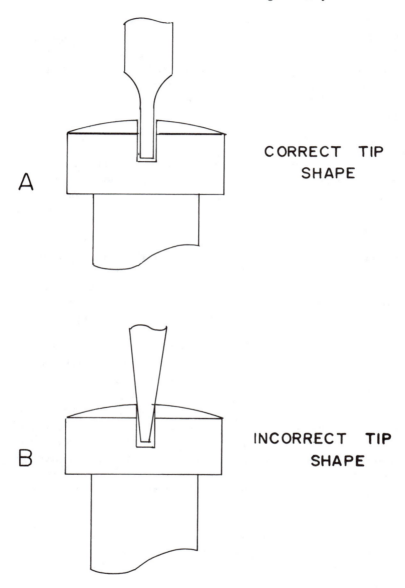

Figure 8. The right and wrong of screwdriver tip shapes suitable for gun work.

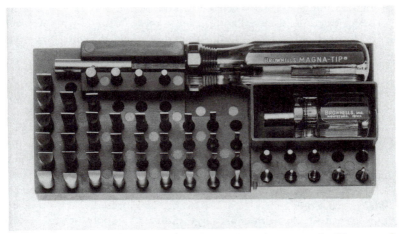

Figure 9. A complete set of screwdriver tips suitable for gun work. (Courtesy of Brownells of Montezuma, Iowa.)

ones most likely to be used routinely. The number- and letter-size drills will be used primarily as tap drills and for drilling holes with proper clearance to accommodate screws. The fractional-size drills are primarily for making holes in general.

Drill Size	*Use*
#38	5-40 tap drill
#37	5-48 tap drill
#36	6-32 tap drill
#33	6-40 tap drill
#31	6-48 tap drill
#30	screw hole drill for #5 screws
#29	8-32 tap drill
#28	8-40 tap drill screw hole drill for #6 screws
#18	screw hole drill for #8 screws
#7	¼"-20 tap drill
#5	¼"-22 tap drill
#3	¼"-25 tap drill
7/32	¼"-28 tap drill
F	screw hole drill for ¼" screws

In addition to the above drills, it would be useful to have an assortment of fractional-size drills in at least ¹⁄₃₂-inch increments in sizes from ¹⁄₁₆ inch to ³⁄₈ inch. All drills should be made of high-speed steel.

TAPS AND DIES

The thread sizes indicated in the twist drill section are those most commonly used in gun work, with the exception of 6-32, 8-32, and ¼-inch-20. These last three, however, have such wide usage and are so common that it is wise to have the tools to produce them. The ¼-22 and ¼-25 are thread sizes for trigger guard screws on some old military rifles. I must confess that even as a full-time professional gunsmith, I rarely used them. Hold off on these until you need them. Most gun screw thread sizes are considered special thread sizes. There was a time when their availability was limited. Now, however, they are available from most large industrial supply houses. Gunsmith supply houses stock just about every size tap and die that could ever be used by the gunsmith.

As a starter, the following sizes are recommended:

Taps	*Dies*
5-40	6-32
6-32	8-32
6-40	¼-20
6-48	
8-32	
8-40	
¼-20	

Note that dies for the strictly gun screw threads are omitted from the above selection. Though it is almost a certainty that you will be required to tap holes for one of these threads, it is far simpler and cheaper to buy ready-made screws in the required sizes than to make your own. Once more, your friendly gunsmith supply houses carry all of the above size screws at a nominal price. The 6-32, 8-32, and ¼-20, on the other hand, will find frequent use for threading gadgetry that may not be a conventional screw.

PRECISION MEASURING TOOLS

If I were limited to just one measuring tool for machine shop work, it would be a 6-inch dial or vernier caliper, preferably the dial caliper, because its numbers are much easier to read and it is faster to use. This instrument can measure within 0.001 inch for thicknesses, outside diameters, inside diameters, and depths up to 6 inches. A 1-inch micrometer is a handy supplement to the dial caliper, if you can afford both. If not, opt for the caliper. A 12-inch steel rule graduated in ⅛-, ¹⁄₃₂-, and ¹⁄₆₄-inch increments is almost a necessity. In addition to its measuring capabilities, it serves as a straightedge.

ELECTRICAL TOOLS

Considering the low price and availability of the electric hand drill, it's surprising that the manual hand drill is still made. Regardless of your ultimate goal, you should have at least a ⅜-inch electric drill. There are currently many imported drill presses available at reasonable prices. Some are junk, but many are serviceable tools. It is possible to buy a ½-inch drill press for less than $200. If this is within your budget, go for it.

The electric bench grinder is another necessity now within the economic reach of most people. A ⅓-horsepower grinder will serve most home workshop needs.

MISCELLANEOUS

Pliers, clamps, punches, scribes, and a multitude of other general and special-use tools fall into this category. You can never get enough of this handy gadgetry, but you can also get by with very little. A pair of combination pliers, long needle nose, and channel lock tongue-and-groove pliers should serve for almost all anticipated needs. A pair of 3-inch toolmakers' clamps comes in handy for such jobs as drilling, tapping, and soldering. For general clamping, a couple of sets of 4-inch C clamps are extremely useful. A scribe may either be purchased or made from a heavy needle cemented into an old toothbrush handle. Figure 2 in chapter 2 shows a set of prick punches and a set of center punches. Frankly, one prick punch and one center punch are about all you'll ever need. A tap wrench is, of course, a necessity.

The file is considered such an important tool that a future chapter will cover its use and will recommend a starter selection. A future chapter will also cover abrasives, hones, and abrasive cloth and paper.

4

Metals

The perfect steel would be one that is easy to machine in its annealed (soft) state and that takes on an excellent finish. When heat-treated it would be super-hard and have exceptional tensile strength, tremendous impact resistance and toughness, and incredible wear resistance at any temperature. It would hold its size and shape when heat-treated. In addition, it would be inexpensive and totally resistant to rust and corrosion. There are some modern steels working toward this end, but they have a long way to go before reaching perfection. By the addition of various alloying ingredients, such as molybdenum, chromium, vanadium, nickel, and carbon, all the properties of the basic iron are altered to some extent to arrive at a desired end. Heat-treating variations will affect the final outcome of any steel. When initially hardened, the steel will be extremely hard and quite brittle because of the internal stresses set up by the hardening process. To relieve these stresses and consequent brittleness, the steel is reheated in a process called tempering. The tempering process relieves stresses and decreases the brittleness. It also softens the steel. The degree of both depends on how high the tempering temperature is raised.

STEEL DESIGNATIONS

Obviously, there are a large number of variables involved in selecting the proper steel for a specific job. Arms manufacturers and custom rifle barrel and action makers employ experts in metallurgy, backed by sophisticated testing equipment, to make the proper choice. The quality of the product and the safety of the shooter demand that the right choice be made. The vast majority of gunsmiths do not make their own barrels and actions. They do, however, install barrels on actions. Though the expertise of a metallurgist is not necessary to execute a proper selection of both, a solid working knowledge of the properties of steel is necessary. It would be courting disaster to install a mild carbon steel barrel designed for a .22 rimfire cartridge on a high-powered rifle action and chamber it for a high-intensity cartridge, such as a .22-.250. Conversely, mild carbon steel will serve quite well in many gun parts not concerned with containing the tremendous forces encountered when a cartridge is fired. It would be economically foolish to use expensive alloy steels for these parts.

Steel begins its life as iron ore, an oxide that contains anywhere from 35 to 60 percent iron. The remaining content is phosphorus, sulfur, silica, and other impurities. After smelting, it is reduced to pig iron with a content of about 92 percent iron, 4 percent carbon, and the remainder, various impurities. This pig iron is the basis of tool steel, both carbon steel and alloy steel. The pig iron is usually mixed with high-grade scrap steel and further refined. The alloying process then takes place. In a chemical analysis of any steel, the percentage of alloying ingredients by weight is always given. These are usually quite small in comparison to the overall composition. The percentage of the major ingredient is never given. This ingredient is iron, regardless of the name given to the final product.

Because of the wide variety of compositions with various alloys and variations in the percentage of their content, a number system permitting identification of various steels was established. The number usually consists of four or five digits, with the first digit identifying the class of steel, the second digit giving the percentage of the major alloying metal, and the last two or three digits giving the percentage of carbon in hundredths of a percent:

1xxx	carbon steel
2xxx	nickel steel

3xxx	nickel chromium
4xxx	molybdenum
5xxx	chromium
6xxx	chromium vanadium
7xxx	tungsten

One of the more common steels used in the gunsmith shop is carbon steel. The first designating digit in the series of four, 1, indicates the class: carbon steel. A combination of the first two digits, 10, indicates that this is a plain carbon steel. The remaining digits indicate the percentage of carbon content in hundredths of a percent. As an example, let's take a 1040 steel. This would indicate a plain carbon steel with 0.40 percent carbon content. To the inexperienced, this quick analysis could be misleading because it appears to indicate that the composition is only iron and carbon. A detailed analysis would indicate the following composition: about 0.50 percent to 0.60 percent manganese, about 0.04 percent phosphorus, about 0.05 percent sulfur, about 0.40 percent carbon, and the remainder, about 99 percent iron. Although manganese is present in a greater percentage than carbon, the steel is still considered a plain carbon steel. Carbon has the greatest influence on the steel. The percentage of carbon content will determine strength, wearability, and whether or not the steel can be hardened. (The sulfur and phosphorus are considered impurities.)

CARBON STEEL USES

Plain carbon steels range in carbon content from about 0.06 percent to about 1.3 percent. The group from 1006 to 1015 are very mild steels and used where strength is not a vital issue. They are ductile and can be worked cold. The group from 1016 to 1020 are considered low carbon steel. The higher carbon content gives them a somewhat greater strength and hardness than the previously described group, at a loss of ductility. These steels machine well and can be case-hardened. They are much used in gun work for such noncritical parts as screws , trigger guards, sling swivels, magazines, butt plates, and grip caps. The medium carbon steels range from 1030 to 1050. With the increase in carbon comes an increase in strength and hardness. Although any of these steels with a carbon content over 0.30 percent can be hardened to some extent, it's not until the composition goes over

0.50 percent carbon that appreciable hardening occurs. Any of these steels can be used for the same purposes as the low carbon steels. Numerous .22-caliber rimfire guns and other older guns chambered for low-pressure cartridges were made from steels in this category. The 1050 to 1095 group is the high carbon tool steel. As the carbon content is increased, there is a corresponding increase in the steel's ability to be hardened. The steel reaches its maximum hardness capability at about 0.80 percent carbon. Beyond this point, resistance to wear increases with the addition of more carbon. A steel with 0.80 percent carbon or more can achieve file hardness. This grade of steel can be used for such things as springs, triggers, firing pins, extractors, hammers, and linkages. Properly heat-treated, it has been used for barrels and actions in high-powered firearms, although the trend now is toward alloy steels. Formerly, high carbon tool steel found much use in the shop for cutting tools because of its hardness and ability to take a keen edge. Unfortunately, as it heats up because of friction caused by the cutting action, it loses its temper, hardness, and cutting edge. It has been generally replaced by more modern steels for this purpose. The highest carbon content seldom exceeds 1.3 percent. Beyond this point, the high level of carbon makes heat-treatment difficult.

HEAT-TREATING TERMINOLOGY

The terms *heat treating* and *hardening* have been used in previous paragraphs without explanation. When heat is applied to steel and the steel is then cooled to atmospheric temperature, a change in its properties takes place. The amount of heat applied and the rate of cooling determine what change takes place. This process can harden the steel, temper it, or anneal it.

HARDENING

Hardening steel takes place in two steps: first, the steel is heated to some temperature above its transformation point (called decalescence point), and second, the steel is cooled suddenly before its new structure can resume its former condition. For carbon steels, the following temperatures usually give good results:

carbon content 0.50 to 0.80	1,450°–1,550°F
carbon content 0.80 to 0.95	1,410°–1,460°F
carbon content 0.95 to 1.10	1,390°–1,430°F

The cooling medium, or quench, used for carbon steel is usually brine. This is about three-quarters of a pound of rock salt per gallon of water. Pure water is not a very satisfactory quench because of its tendency to bubble and form a vapor barrier around the hot steel. The result is uneven cooling, causing uneven stresses in the steel and possible cracking.

TEMPERING

When the steel is hardened, it is extremely hard and brittle and contains internal stresses caused by the sudden cooling in the quenching bath. The purpose of tempering, or drawing, is to remove the internal stresses and reduce the brittleness. Tempering will also soften the hardened steel to a certain extent. The process is similar to hardening, in that the hardened steel is reheated and then cooled. On reheating to some temperature between 300° and 750°F, the hardened steel assumes a softer and tougher structure than in its hardened state. When cooled to atmosphere temperature, it retains this structure. The temperature range for tempering carbon steel is narrow, and fairly exacting temperatures are required for different applications.

ANNEALING

The purpose of annealing is to soften the steel and relieve internal stresses. The steel is heated to a temperature in the critical range, held at that temperature for a while, then slowly cooled to atmosphere temperature. In the gunsmith shop, the primary purpose of this process is to soften the steel so that it can be machined.

CASE HARDENING

Low carbon steel cannot be hardened by the methods described above because of its low carbon content. It can, however, be given an almost glasslike hardness on its surface if heated to a temperature of about 1,500°F in the presence of a carbonaceous material and then rapidly quenched. As the carbonaceous material decomposes because of the heat, it releases carbon, which is absorbed by the surface of the steel. The longer the two remain together in the presence of heat, the deeper the case. The depth of the case usually goes from about 0.008 to 0.015 inches. The 1015 to 1020 plain carbon steels are most suitable for case hardening. This process gives an extremely hard surface and a soft, tough inner core to the steel. It finds much use in the gun shop.

Different steels require different rates of cooling in the hardening process. Plain carbon steel, for instance, is a water-hardening steel. This means that it must be cooled rapidly to harden. If a small piece of 1080 with a diameter of $3/16$ inch, for example, were heated to its hardening temperature and quenched in brine, it would be hard clear through. A piece of the steel with the same analysis but 1 inch in diameter, heat-treated in the same manner, would harden only to a depth of about $1/8$ inch. The core would be soft and tough. If both pieces were quenched in oil the smaller piece would still probably be hardened clear through. The larger piece would be soft clear through. The explanation is the rate of cooling. Brine is a rapid-cooling medium. The smaller piece of steel is cooled in its entirety rapidly enough to harden. The larger piece, on the other hand, is cooled rapidly on the surface, but the heat in its interior cannot be liberated fast enough to permit hardening clear through. Oil, being a slower-cooling medium, fails to cool the larger piece with sufficient speed to permit any hardening. As can be seen, mass plays an important part in the process. This phenomenon of a hard exterior and soft, tough interior is desirable in many applications. One of the disadvantages of water-hardening steel is that the rapid cooling tends to distort. In intricate parts, this could be a major problem.

The addition of certain alloys to the carbon tool steel creates a situation where the steel hardens so rapidly that a rapid cooling is no longer critical. As a matter of fact, quenching this type of steel in brine would most likely cause it to crack. This type is known as oil-hardening steel. It is deep hardening, usually hardening clear through. One of its big advantages is that it comes through the hardening process with less distortion and shrinkage and is less susceptible to cracks and fractures caused by the internal stresses of more rapid cooling.

An even more rapidly hardening steel than oil hardening is air hardening. The quench is air. Because of its low cooling rate, distortion, shrinkage, and internal stresses are even less than with oil-hardening steel.

HOME HEAT TREATING

The requirements for heat treating are a source of heat, a method of determining temperature, and a quenching bath. A modern heat-treating furnace will efficiently handle the first two requirements. The furnace temperature is easily preset and, once reached, accurately maintained. Unfortunately, these furnaces are expensive, and only the larger shops doing a considerable amount of heat treating can afford them. A quench for occasional home heat treating presents very few problems. A lightweight, nondetergent motor oil will do for oil-hardening, and three-quarters of a pound of rock salt per gallon of water will serve for water hardening. Make sure that the volume is sufficient to absorb and dissipate all of the heat from the steel.

Two sources of heat usually available in the average home are the kitchen stove and the small, hand-held propane torch. (If you don't have a propane torch, they're available in any hardware store for around $10.) The combination, properly employed, can serve adequately as the heat sources for home heat-treating. The propane torch flame develops a temperature of about 2,300°F. With MAP gas, a considerably higher temperature can be reached. Although these temperatures far exceed anything needed for the hardening temperature, the size of the flame is usually too small to provide sufficient heat to heat anything but the smallest parts uniformly. The point at which the flame is applied can be heated to red-hot, but the red heat will not spread to the rest of the part because the surrounding atmosphere dissipates the heat more rapidly than it can be applied. The problem, then, is to contain most of the heat in a small area around the part being treated, thus the oven.

A simple, serviceable oven can easily be fashioned from fire brick, available at most heating and plumbing supply houses. On a piece of sheet metal, lay two firebricks side by side, with the long edges touching (figure 10). Using four firebricks, form a box just larger than the part to be heated upon the base. Leave space at the edges so air can get inside and support combustion. One brick should have two holes chiseled through its long face to admit the torch. (I like to use two torches.) Additional firebrick is then laid on top of the open box to complete the containment. Crude, but it works.

Although this oven works quite well for the hardening process, it's not too efficient for tempering. Because of the large amount of heat and the consequent time involved in bringing a part to hardening

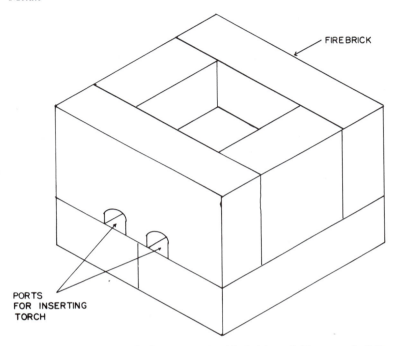

FIREBRICK

PORTS
FOR INSERTING
TORCH

Figure 10. A simple heat-treating oven made of firebrick available at most building supply stores. A single brick is laid over the top to complete the enclosure. Leave enough space between the bricks so that air can get into the chamber and sustain combustion.

temperature, the item can be visually checked periodically to observe its progress. Tempering temperatures, however, are much lower and require much closer control. This is when the kitchen oven comes in handy. The oven in my kitchen can attain a temperature of 550°F. For many applications, this is a sufficiently high tempering temperature. Some jobs and some steels may require a higher temperature. Pure lead melts at 620°F. Not too much work will require a temperature higher than that.

Determining the temperature of heated steel without suitable instrumentation can be done by observing the color changes the steel goes through as it is heated. The color and temperature equivalents given here are fairly standard, although some charts may differ by 10°F, plus or minus.

Color of Steel	Temperature
pale yellow	430°F
light yellow	440°F
pale straw	450°F
straw	460°F
deep straw	470°F
yellow brown	490°F
brown yellow	500°F
light purple	530°F
dark purple	550°F
dark blue	570°F
light blue	620°F
faint red	930°F
blood red	1,075°F
cherry	1,375°F
bright cherry	1,450°F
salmon	1,550°F
lemon	1,830°F
white	2,200°F

It takes considerable experience and practice to attain proficiency in judging temperatures by color. The amount and type of light in the room and the individual's eyesight and perception of what the stated color should look like all play important roles. One man's bright cherry might be salmon to another. The above method might be suitable for the village smithy, but there is a much more simple and accurate method available for the aspiring gunsmith. A paint-type substance called Tempilaq (available from Brownells, Montezuma, Iowa) is thinly painted on the part to be heat-treated. The part is then heated. When the temperature is reached corresponding to the designated Tempilaq temperature, the Tempilaq will immediately melt. This liquid is available for temperatures from 400°F to 1,550°F in sufficient temperature increments to accommodate any heat-treating situation. Tempilaq should be used even when tempering in the kitchen oven. The oven temperature control may be set at 500°F, but chances are the actual oven temperature will be something different. Discrepancies of 20° to 25° from the dial settings of older ovens are not unusual.

As explained earlier, case hardening is a process whereby carbon is transferred from some compound in contact with the low carbon steel to its surface in sufficient quantity to permit the steel to have a hard case when quenched in brine. There are several methods and numerous compounds available to execute this process. One chemical commonly used in industry is sodium cyanide. Unless you are thoroughly versed in use and handling of cyanide and have all the proper equipment, *do not attempt to use cyanide.* The least little mishap can result in instant death from poisoning. Other compounds available under various brand names are quite effective and safe to use. (Brownells, of Montezuma, Iowa, is a good source of supply.)

All case-hardening compounds come with manufacturer's instructions for use. Although there might be some small variations between different brands, essentially the procedures are the same. For the small parts normally case-hardened by the gunsmith, the part is heated to a temperature of about 1,500°F, dipped in the compound until it acquires a good coating, reheated, and then quenched in brine. If a deeper case is required, the procedure is repeated.

5

The File

The file is the oldest tool for the controlled removal of material. The first cavemen to use an ax, spearhead, or knife had to have some way to put a finished edge on their weapon. This was probably another stone, rougher and harder, used in a manner similar to filing. Through the bronze and iron ages, the refinement of the file advanced. The teeth were cut into the metal by manually striking a chisel at the proper angle, to the proper depth, uniformly spaced. Unearthed by archaeologists, iron files dating back before the time of Christ bear a striking resemblance to the modern file. They have both shapes and cuts similar to modern files. Usable, albeit crude.

The practice of cutting the teeth manually with the hammer and chisel probably continued into the mid-eighteenth century. Although Leonardo da Vinci sketched a Rube Goldberg contraption for cutting file teeth as early as 1490, there is no evidence that it was ever made or used. Information on who actually made and put the first file-cutting machine into practical commercial use is contradictory and confusing. It is generally acknowledged that after the mid-eighteenth century there were a number of machines in use producing files. Most skilled craftsmen and artisans, however, required files of shapes and precision that the machines of that era could not produce, so they cut their own files by hand. F. L. Grobet, a Swiss toolmaker, is credited with designing and building the first machine capable of cutting precision, uniform files in 1836.

The metals used for making files probably had a more rapid evolution than the actual mechanics involved. No sooner had a better material been discovered than it was used as a file material. The evolution proceeded from bronze to iron to mild steel with its various methods of carburizing the teeth to make them harder than the base metal. Until recently, carbon tool steel was the material of which modern files were made. Today, carbon steel is being replaced by special alloy steels that are superior for working on the various modern metals used by industry.

The file of today is truly a precision metal-removal tool of the highest state of development. There are a shape, size, and cut available for just about any job. In addition to files made of conventional steels, there are diamond files that can be used on carbide and hardened steel. The Grobet-Swiss catalog states that their company offers "more than 1,000 types, sizes, and cuts. . . ." Obviously, few shops can stock and use this complete line. The price alone would be about the equivalent of a luxury foreign car. However, anything that the craftsman could possibly use is readily available.

Filing is an art. The file is a hand-held cutting tool, guided only by the hands of the individual doing the filing. In a sense, the mechanic with his file can be compared to a pianist, a sculptor, or a portrait painter. All rely on the movement and dexterity of their arms and hands to produce the final desired result. All must know the instrument, the instrument's capabilities, and the basic fundamentals of its usage. If the basic fundamentals are adhered to and the arms and hands are expertly manipulated, the results will be Horowitz, Rembrandt, and Cellini.

A quote from a brochure of a well-known manufacturer of files: ". . . filing is an art that can be learned only by long and patient practice." Although I agree with everything else in the brochure, I highly disagree with that statement. It has been my experience that mastering the art of filing is not like body-building in preparation for a Mr. Universe contest, where each small gain comes only after long, strenuous hours of weight-lifting. It is more like a child learning to ride a bicycle. After numerous falls, under the watchful eye of Dad, suddenly he or she has got it! Within two or three days the child is riding "no hands." Just about everybody I know whom I consider a master with a file agrees with this assessment. When you've finally got the touch, you know it. From then on, it's coasting downhill. Obviously, as with any discipline, time and experience increase the degree of proficiency. However, mastering the file need not be the slow, painful, evolutionary process that so many make it out to be.

CONSTRUCTION AND CUTS

Figure 11 illustrates a basic shape of a file with terminology applicable to its construction. Note that the length of a file is measured exclusive of the tang. Also shown in an exaggerated scale for illustration are the degrees of coarseness and types of cuts. The coarseness is determined by the spacing and depth of the teeth. Utilizing terminology applicable to American pattern files, there are six grades: rough,

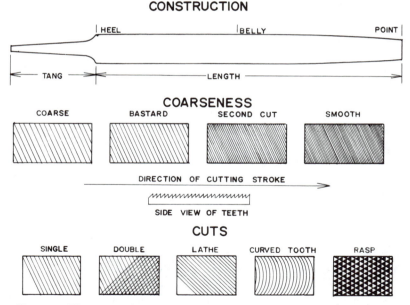

Figure 11. File construction and terminology as applied to American pattern files. Swiss pattern files use the same basic terminology. They are more accurately made, and the coarseness of cut is designated differently.

coarse, bastard, second cut, smooth, and dead smooth. (The rough and dead smooth are now seldom listed in manufacturers' catalogs; the most commonly used American pattern files are the coarse, bastard, second cut, and smooth.) The more teeth per inch, the finer and smoother the cut of the file. The number of teeth per inch for a particular cut will vary for different lengths of the file. For example, a 10-inch bastard will have more teeth per inch than a 12-inch bastard. Consequently, the 12-inch file will have a coarser cut. These same proportions will hold true for the other cuts.

As can be seen from the side view of the teeth shapes in figure 11, the file will cut *only* on the forward stroke. The teeth on a single-cut file are cut in rows parallel to each other at about a 65-degree angle to the long axis of the file. The double-cut file has a second set of teeth, called the upcut, cut over the first series of teeth, called the overcut. The two sets of teeth are at an angle to each other and form a series of diamonds. The second set of teeth (the upcut) is finer than the first series (the overcut). The overcut acts as a chip breaker. The long-angle lathe file is also single-cut. This particular cut is used primarily on rotating work in a lathe. The longer angle of the cut permits more of a shearing cut on the material being filed.

Two other cuts shown in figure 11 are the milled curved tooth and the rasp. The teeth of the curved-tooth file are arranged in curved contours across the length of the file. The convex side of the curved tooth is the cutting side. The teeth have a definite undercut, which permits the file to take a deep bite. The rasp is a pattern of disconnected teeth individually formed by a single pointed tool. The teeth are quite sharp and coarse.

SWISS PATTERN FILES

Swiss pattern files are made to more precise standards than American pattern files. They are narrower and less thick, and the teeth extend to the extreme edges. They are finer and designated differently. Comparable cut designations are as follows:

American Pattern	Swiss Pattern
bastard	No. 00
second cut	No. 0
smooth	No. 2

	cross section	shape	taper	use
Flat		rectangular	tapered	general purpose
Hand		rectangular	uniform	flat surfaces
Pillar		width narrower than hand file	uniform	keyways, slots, narrow work
Warding		thin rectangular	tapered	slots
Square		square	tapered	square corner holes
Three square		triangular	tapered	acute angles, corners
Round		round	tapered or straight	round corners, curved surfaces
Half-round		third circular	tapered	curved surfaces
Knife		knife-shaped	tapered	slots
Equaling		rectangular	uniform	slots, corners
Crochet		flat with round edges	tapered	slots, flat surfaces, round corners
Barrette		trapezoid	tapered	corners, flat surfaces
Cant		triangular	tapered	corners
Slitting		diamond	blunt	slots, corners
Crossing		oval	tapered	rounded surfaces
Pippin		apple seed	tapered	general

Figure 12. Cross-sectional shapes, names, and usage. All are available in Swiss pattern files and many American pattern files. (Courtesy of Simonds Cutting Tools.)

Swiss pattern files range in cut from No. 00 to No. 8. The No. 00 Swiss pattern file (comparable to bastard) in an 8-inch length would have 41 teeth to the inch. A No. 6 Swiss pattern file in an 8-inch length would have 173 teeth per inch. An 8-inch American pattern smooth cut (usually the finest available) would have about 79 teeth per inch. Generally, the teeth of Swiss pattern files are chisel-cut up to No. 2. For files finer than No. 2, the teeth are etched-cut. This is a method of drawing an etching tool across the annealed file blank under pressure.

Swiss pattern files are primarily used for precision finish work. The preciseness of their construction, combined with the wide variety of shapes, sizes, and cuts, make them particularly adaptable to work of such precision craftsmen as toolmakers, die makers, and gunsmiths.

SHAPES

The shape of a file is the view that one gets when looking at a cross section. There are about sixteen basic shapes, each with its own name. Some of the names are logical and relate directly to the cross-sectional shape. Many, however, are rather weird and confusing to the novice. Figure 12 illustrates the sixteen most common shapes and describes their characteristics and general applications. Most of the shapes are common to both the American and Swiss pattern files. As can be seen, there is a shape to accommodate almost any contour. Keep in mind that there are many sizes to each shape.

TYPES

Figure 13 illustrates several commonly used files in American pattern and curved tooth. Those shown in American pattern are also available in Swiss pattern. These are the kinds of files that are familiar to most people and that can probably be found in the home workshop, certainly in most machine shops. They are adaptable to general types of work when size and configuration permit the use of a full or nearly full stroke. The curved tooth files are often used in auto body work. I find they work quite well on mild steel in general when large amounts of metal are to be removed. As a wild guess, perhaps 80 percent of all gun work requiring a file can be handled with the five American pattern files shown. The remaining 20 percent will require files of special sizes and configurations.

Figure 14 illustrates a set of needle files. They are made in most of

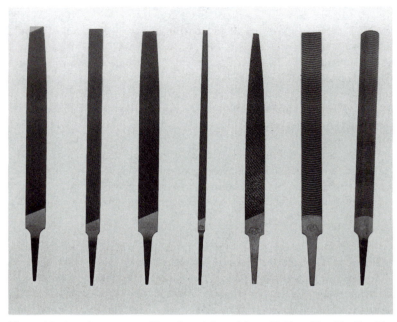

Figure 13. American pattern files. *From left to right:* mill file, pillar file, flat file, square file, warding file, flat curved milled tooth file, half-round curved milled tooth file. (Courtesy of Grobet File Co.)

the shapes shown in figure 12. Needle files come in lengths from 4 inches to 7¾ inches, overall length. All are Swiss pattern and come in cuts from No. 00 to No. 6. They are used for applications similar to larger tang files, but on a smaller scale and where fine precision filing is required. They are commonly used by toolmakers and die makers and find much use in the gunsmith shop.

The term *riffler*, as defined in Grobet-Swiss literature, is derived from the German word *riefeln*, meaning to channel, chaufer, flute, or groove. In the world of files, it applies to a specialized type of file used by toolmakers, die sinkers, silversmiths, wood carvers, and just about any skilled artisan engaged in similar work. The Grobet-Swiss catalog illustrates 89 kinds of rifflers available in a variety of sizes and cuts ranging from No. 0 to No. 6. They are available in all of the cross-sectional shapes shown in figure 12 and some shapes not shown.

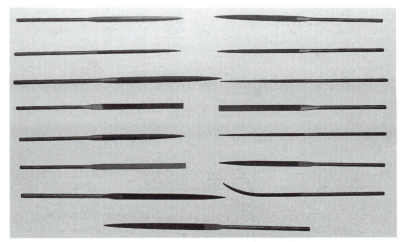

Figure 14. Swiss pattern needle files. *Top to bottom left:* barrette, crochet, crossing, equalling, joint, knife, marking. *Top to bottom left:* marking, oval, round, slitting, square, three square, three square bent. *Bottom center:* warding. (Courtesy of Grobet File Co.)

Figure 15 illustrates a few of the more oddly configured diesinkers' rifflers. Figure 16 shows a set of toolmakers' rifflers. These rifflers are just a larger version of diesinkers' rifflers, and the same configurations are available in the smaller size.

The riffler has the same configuration, shape, and cut on each end. The length of the cut is short in relation to the overall length. The

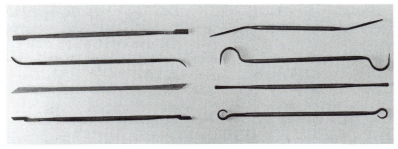

Figure 15. Diesinkers' rifflers. All are 6 inches long, Swiss pattern. These are some of the odder configurations. (Courtesy of Grobet File Co.)

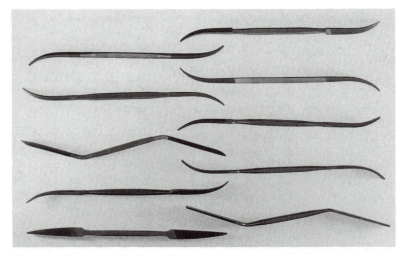

Figure 16. Toolmakers' rifflers. All are 12 inches long, Swiss pattern. They are available in most cross-sectional shapes. (Courtesy of Grobet File Co.)

middle body serves as the handle. The large selection of configurations, shapes, and sizes permits the use of rifflers in otherwise restricted, hard-to-reach areas. As a matter of fact, it would be difficult to come up with a situation requiring precision filing for which a riffler is not available.

FILING

There are four basic types of filing: straight, draw, lathe, and precision. In straight filing the file is pushed straight across the work, making its cut on the forward (or pushed) stroke. It is returned to the starting position in a slightly raised position so as not to touch the work, and the forward (cutting) stroke is repeated. This procedure is repeated until the desired results are reached. In draw filing the tip of the file is held in one hand; the heel is held in the other. The file is moved across the work in a direction perpendicular to the long axis of the file. For purposes of this book lathe filing has no application, so it will not be covered. Precision filing covers a multitude of operations ranging from finish-filing a flat surface to the use of rifflers in small, restricted areas. General application of this category will be covered.

Since most work to be filed is relatively small, logic dictates that it be held in a vise. The vise should be at such a height that the top of the work will be at elbow height when the arm is extended for filing. The work must be held securely, and the bench must be solid and rigid, or chattering will result. Chattering occurs when the work moves while the file is moving across. The file teeth become momentarily disengaged from their cutting action, and as the file proceeds along its stroke, a series of vibrations is set up. The resulting noise needs no explanation. The filed surface, as a consequence of the chatter, is ragged. This situation will also cause damage to the file.

STRAIGHT FILING HAND GRIPS

The positions and procedures covered will apply to right-hand filing. If you're left-handed, simply reverse the hands and follow the same procedures. There are four basic hand grips for straight filing: normal filing for average stock (metal) removal, heavy stock removal, flat filing, and precision filing. The right hand grips the handle of the file in the same manner for all four situations. The handle is held in the palm of the right hand with the thumb extended along the top of the handle. For normal stock removal, the tip of the file is held in the left hand with the tip of the thumb pressing on top of the file and the forefinger and second finger curled around the point (figure 17A). For heavy stock removal, the thumb of the left hand is placed on the forward part of the file, in line with the axis of the file. All four fingers are then curled around the file. This provides a powerful grip and permits the application of heavy pressure on the file. Heavy stock removal using this grip is usually accomplished more efficiently when the workpiece is somewhat lower than for the other grips (figure 17B).

Often it is necessary to clean up a surface that is already flat and does not need much stock removal. An example would be a newly machined surface where it is necessary to remove only the machine marks left by the cutting tool. The positioning of the left hand in this case would be with the thumb and fingers spread as far apart as possible, the thumb placed toward the rear of the file and the fingers toward the point. Equal pressure is applied by both the thumb and the fingers (figure 17C). This assures even pressure along the length of the file, and any tendency to rock the file can readily be detected.

Precision two-handed filing requires minimal stock removal and

Figure 17. For efficiency and accuracy, hold the file as shown in these photographs. *A*, Left-hand grip for normal filing. *B*, Left-hand grip for heavy stock removal. *C*, Left-hand position for flat filing. *D*, Left-hand grip for two-handed precision filing.

close control of the file. The tip of the file should be held between the thumb and forefinger (figure 17*D*) of the left hand. This grip provides for both file control and pressure control.

STRAIGHT FILING

The filer should stand facing the work, feet 18 to 20 inches apart, with the left foot 6 to 8 inches ahead of the right foot. The workpiece is approximately opposite the right shoulder. The position should be such as to obtain a free swing from the shoulders. Utilizing any of the grips described above, the file is pushed across the material being filed. The stroke should be such that the file proceeds at a moderate speed, with even overall pressure, in a flat plane. On the return stroke, the file should be lifted slightly, to clear the workpiece. It should never touch the work on the return stroke. As stated earlier, files are constructed to cut only on the forward stroke. Contact with the work on the return stroke will rapidly dull the file. Rocking the file is a major fault with novices. This rocking, or seesaw, effect will produce a convex surface. It must be remembered that as the stroke begins, most of the file and the handle are away from the workpiece and almost totally under the control of the right hand. Because of the enormous leverage involved, there is a natural tendency to depress the rear of the file below the plane of the work being filed. As the stroke proceeds beyond the file midpoint, the tendency is reversed and the left hand assumes the dominant controlling force. A conscious effort must be made to vary the pressures with each hand as the stroke proceeds to keep the file in a straight plane.

It is virtually impossible to describe the amount of pressure to exert on the file in concrete pounds per square inch terms. The best that can be said is, don't use too much, or too little. This is an aspect of hand filing involving the feel. When you've got it, you know it! Too little pressure will not remove metal in a smooth, cutting action. It will just scratch up the surface and dull the file. Too much pressure will result in too much metal being removed, which will clog the file teeth, cause "pinning" (particles firmly embedded in the file teeth), gouge the workpiece, and dull the file. Additionally, different grades of coarseness, different file cuts and lengths, and different metals all have different pressure requirements.

Precisely what is this "feel" or "touch" referred to in several places throughout this chapter? When you are exerting the proper pressure at the proper cutting stroke speed and producing a smooth cut, you feel it. When the pressure is too light, you will feel it. When pressure is too heavy and pinning and clogging occur and the work is being scored, you'll feel it. The feel is indescribable, but you'll know it when you feel it.

STRAIGHT FILING EXERCISES

The stories of the old-time apprentice beginning his apprenticeship by filing the perfect cube have too often been regarded as just that: stories and folklore. I've known a couple of toolmakers who often recited this story as part of their early training. My father-in-law, who began his apprenticeship in 1915, was one of them. He was World

Class with a file. Some years ago I tried this perfect cube exercise and felt that it had much merit and was perhaps the quickest path to becoming proficient with a file.

Select a piece of mild steel of approximately rectangular shape and of a size that could produce a perfect 1-inch cube. Using a hacksaw, trim it down to a rough cube of about 1⅛-inch dimensions. The first step in creating the perfect cube is to establish a perfect reference plane. With the cube held firmly in a vise, begin filing with either a 12- or a 14-inch, bastard, double-cut flat file. The object of this first filing operation is not to remove a large amount of material and arrive at the proper dimension, but to get a perfect plane, as nearly square as possible with its adjacent planes. Utilizing the left-hand grip for normal stock removal, commence filing. After filing for a number of strokes in a given direction, alter the direction (either left or right) across the workpiece by about 45 degrees. The new file marks, from the altered direction, superimposed on the old file marks will give an indication of any area neglected or too heavily favored. After a number of strokes, alter the direction about 90 degrees in the opposite direction. This will give an even better indication of the area's contact. When it appears that the whole surface has been covered and looks flat, remove the cube from the vise and check the surface with a straightedge. Holding the cube up toward a strong light, lay the straightedge diagonally across the filed surface using one set of opposing corners, and then the other set. Check across the length of all four sides with the straightedge.

Don't be disappointed if your first effort did not produce a perfect flat. It would be miraculous if it had. Mark the high spots with a red crayon. Now, using either a machinists' square or combination square, check to ensure that your flat is approximately square with the adjoining four sides. If it is too far off, concentrate on the high side or sides. Return the cube to the vise and resume filing until the surface is flat and approximately square with the other four sides. Concentrate on pushing the file stroke in a straight line and avoiding rocking. Repeat the flatness and squareness checks with the straightedge and square periodically. Eventually you'll arrive at an acceptable reference plane. Finish up your filing on this plane with a 10-inch second cut mill file, using the left-hand grip for flat filing.

The second and third flats will also be reference planes. These two flats will be adjoining each other and the first flat you filed. Employ the same procedures on these two as for the first flat. Now, however, you must file them perfectly square with each other, in addition to being perfectly flat.

Assuming that the first three flats have been filed flat and square with each other, we are now ready to bring the cube to its finished dimensions. Mark these flats with a red crayon so you won't confuse them with the remaining sides later. From now on, they are strictly reference planes and will not be subjected to any further filing. Select an unfiled side, and paint the four sides adjoining it for about ¼ inch below that side with lay-out fluid. Using the finished flat opposite as your reference, scribe a line around the cube 1 inch from the reference flat. This scribed line will act as a guide while filing. Resume filing as described above. As you approach the scribed line, begin your measurements of the two opposing flats using your dial or vernier caliper. The dial or vernier has the added advantage of having perfectly parallel jaws. With one set held flush against the reference surface, it is quite simple to check for flatness and squareness with the other set. When you are within about + 0.005 inch of your required final dimension, shift to the 10-inch second cut mill file and begin flat filing. Repeat the procedure for the other two sides. It is a certainty that by the time you finish your perfect cube you will have developed the touch or feel. Don't expect to complete the project in one continuous effort. You'll miss a lot of meals and sleep if you try. Allot about an hour a day for filing. Depending on your concentration and dedication, it should be completed well within a month and you will be on the way to becoming an expert with a file. The two other types of filing described in the chapter use the same basic principles, the feel is the same, and you'll find them relatively simple to perform.

DRAW FILING

This type of filing is used primarily to produce smooth, level surfaces on planes and edges. Generally, the length of the work is much greater than work that would employ straight filing. Although the method is used primarily to produce a flat surface, it finds much use in the removal of rust pits on round gun barrels being prepared for polishing.

All manufacturers' instruction booklets on filing that I have read describe the procedure in identical terms, almost verbatim. Most young men that I have observed entering the shop for the first time are obviously taught the same procedures in machinist school. The orthodox method certainly works and produces excellent results.

The file used for draw filing is usually a single-cut mill file or a long-angle lathe file. It is held so that the long axis of the file is at a right angle to the direction of the stroke. The tang area is held in the right hand, and the tip area is held in the left hand (figure 18*A*). The thumbs are on the top of the file, pointed inward. The hands should be on the file as close to the work as possible. This will permit better control and lessen the tendency to rock the file. The file is alternately pushed and pulled across the face of the workpiece, with an even pressure on both the push and pull stroke.

The principle behind draw filing is that the file teeth are at such a cutting angle as to produce a shearing cut rather than a straight cut, as with straight filing. Much less pinning is encountered in draw filing. The result is almost always a fine surface finish. Although I have used the above method on occasion and found it to produce excellent results, I do find fault with it. File teeth cut only in one direction. In the above procedures, the file will cut only on the push stroke. Since the return, or pull stroke, produces no cutting action, there is no logic in maintaining pressure on the file.

Many years ago I was taught a method almost the opposite of the one just described. The tang area is held in the left hand, and the tip area is held in the right hand (figure 18*B*). The stroke begins in the far end of the work (away from the filer) and the file is drawn toward the filer. On the return stroke, the file is lifted off the work, returned to the starting position, and the stroke is repeated. I have found it easier to maintain control of the file while it is being drawn rather than being pushed. Additionally, by setting the file down on the work prior to each cutting stroke, there is a conscious effort to maintain an even pressure on the file throughout the stroke. This reduces the tendency to apply maximum pressure in the middle of the stroke as is common with the push-pull method earlier described. The finish produced by this method always seems to be finer.

PRECISION FILING

Two-handed precision filing with larger tang files was covered earlier. This section will pertain to the smaller files such as needle files and rifflers. Most filing using these files will be done with one hand. As with the larger files, the stroke is the same: Cut only on the

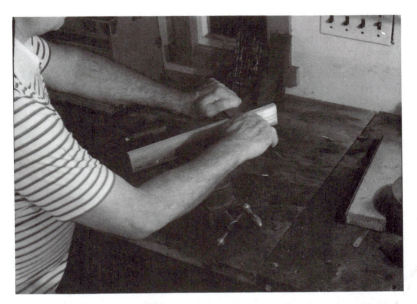

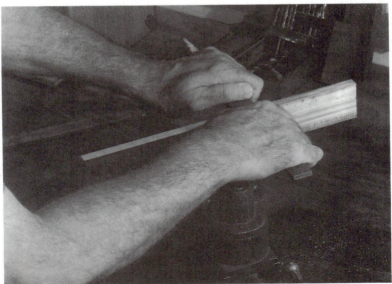

Figure 18. The object of draw filing is to produce a shearing cut. *A*, Conventional draw-filing grip. *B*, Author's modified draw-filing grip.

forward stroke. The needle files have tangs that often serve as handles. Having had file tangs deeply pierce the palm of my hand on several occasions, I am leery of any file with a tang and without a handle. On my needle files, I use a pin vise with a collet as a handle. In addition to the obvious safety feature, the handle provides better control. The method of holding the file that works best for me is similar to the right-hand grip for straight filing, except that the hand is rotated 90 degrees counterclockwise. The thumb ends up on the left-hand side of the handle, and the forefinger is on top of the file body. The forefinger regulates the pressure on the file and serves to guide it. For really delicate filing, the file is held like a pencil or pen.

The larger rifflers, such as toolmakers' and silversmiths' rifflers, are held similar to the needle files, with the forefinger on top of the body. Smaller rifflers are held like a pencil or pen.

FILE CARE

The file is a precision cutting tool and should be handled as such. Files should never be carelessly thrown in a drawer or toolbox where they can bang against each other. As diamonds cut diamonds, so one file striking another will cause damage to the teeth. Either drill holes through the handles so that you can hang the files on pegs, or hang them up with spring clips as described in chapter 3. Needle files and rifflers usually come with plastic cases and should be stored in them.

Files become rapidly clogged when in use. Usually a file card brushed along the angle of the teeth will remove the metal filings. Often the file will become pinned. Use a heavy-gauge needle or a similar sharp instrument to remove the particles. Never continue filing with a pinned file; it will just gouge up your work. Rubbing chalk across the face of the file reduces the tendency to pin. On files of No. 2 or finer, a file card is usually too coarse to clean out the teeth. I have found that a tool made of a heavy putty knife sharpened to a keen edge across the end works extremely well. Position the sharpened edge perpendicular to the file teeth, with the knife at about a 60-degree angle to the file. Apply a moderate amount of force to the putty knife, and move it in the direction of the file teeth. The teeth will actually imprint on the knife edge, permitting it to mesh with them. Works real well.

FILE SELECTION

As stated earlier, there are a file size, shape, cut, and configuration for any situation that the average gunsmith, toolmaker, or die maker could encounter in three lifetimes. However, quality files are expensive, and it would probably take three lifetimes to pay for all of them. You will soon discover how few you can really get by with. As a starter set, the following files are recommended:

- 12-inch flat, double cut, bastard
- 12-inch mill bastard
- 10-inch second cut, mill file
- 10-inch round, bastard
- 12-inch half round, bastard
- 6-inch half round, bastard

All of the above files are in American pattern. For Swiss pattern files, a set of twelve to fifteen needle files in 6-inch length, No. 0 cut, should be sufficient to start with. There is usually no need for rifflers at this stage. When you feel that you need them, select the size, shape, and configuration most appropriate for the job from a manufacturer's catalog.

Summary: It may appear that unusually large coverage was given to one tool—the file. However, it is the file that will produce the final shapes and dimensions of your work. Mastery of the basic outlines in this chapter will make the projects in future chapters not only feasible but almost routine.

6

Abrasives

The modern grinding wheel is millions of small cutting tools bonded together into a wheel by one of several bonding agents. As its periphery passes over the surface of the substance being ground, the surface layer of abrasive cuts away material in a manner similar to any metallic cutting tool. This cutting action is the same for abrasive paper or cloth and hones.

The mass introduction of abrasives into industry during this century has done as much to advance technological progress as the refinement and development of conventional metal-removal machine tools. (Some say even more.) Abrasives in one form or another can be used to remove fairly large amounts of metal for rough work. The same abrasive can be used to impart a super-accurate, super-fine finish far beyond the capabilities of metallic metal-removal tools. Where a tolerance of one-thousandth of an inch is practical for the lathe or milling machine, tolerances in the millionths of an inch are possible for abrasives. Abrasives do not recognize hardness in any material. A workpiece that is too hard to be machined by conventional cutting tools poses no problem for the proper abrasive.

A substance known as emery was used in a loose granular form for various polishing and grinding functions for centuries. Sometime in the 1840s emery grains were sized and bonded with clay to form the emery grinding wheel. Sized, loose emery grains were glued to paper or cloth to produce a tool for polishing metal. For years the term *emery* was the only term used when referring to a wheel or to paper or cloth. Even today the layman will refer to any grinding wheel or abrasive cloth used on metal as an emery wheel or emery cloth, even though it is most likely not emery. Although there are still numerous applications in which emery finds much use, this natural substance has largely been replaced by man-made abrasives. Being a product of nature, emery is characterized by a lack of uniformity and quality. Artificial abrasives, on the other hand, can be closely controlled in each stage of production.

SILICON CARBIDE

In the early 1890s a process was developed for synthesizing a better abrasive than the naturally occurring emery. In simple terms, sand and carbon were subjected to an extremely high temperature. The result was silicon carbide. Very pure glass sand (pure white quartz) and ground coke are mixed with varying amounts of salt and sawdust. The mixture is heated in an electric furnace to a temperature in excess of 4,000°F for about thirty-six hours. After cooling, the uncombined mixture is removed and the remaining result is a mass of silicon carbide. The large lumps of silicon carbide are then crushed into small grains, further refined, and sized.

ALUMINUM OXIDE

In the late 1890s another man-made abrasive was developed from bauxite. Bauxite, as it occurs in nature, is an impure aluminum oxide. (Aluminum oxide is the cutting ingredient in emery.) The bauxite is mixed with ground coke and iron filings. The mixture is heated to a high temperature in an electric furnace and fused into a glassy mass. When cooled, the mass is crushed, refined, and sized. The result is aluminum oxide of about 96 percent purity.

Silicon carbide and aluminum oxide are the two most widely used abrasives today. Although there are several modern developments approaching and even equaling the hardness of the diamond, including artificial diamonds, they are relatively expensive and find their usage in highly specialized work. Each abrasive has its own general applications. Aluminum oxide is superior to silicon carbide for use on high-tensile-strength materials, such as alloy steels, high-speed steel, and carbon steel. Silicon carbide, on the other hand, performs better on low-tensile-strength materials, such as copper, aluminum, brass, and nonmetallic materials. A special grade of silicon carbide, green in color, can be used to grind extremely hard, brittle materials, such as carbide tools.

The abrasive grains cut the metal being ground, lapped, honed, or sanded. Tiny chips of metal are removed. The next time you are around a shop grinder and happen to have a small magnet in your pocket, pass the magnet over the residue from past grinding operations. Much of the residue is loose abrasive from the wheel. Much of it, however, will cling to your magnet as tiny steel chips removed by the grinding operations. The size of the metal chips is subject to control during the manufacture of the wheel. Coarse abrasive grains will remove larger chips and give a consequently rougher finish. Conversely, finer abrasive grains will produce smaller chips and a smoother finish. Abrasive grain size, or grit, is determined by the size of screen-mesh the grains will pass through. Grain sizes run from about 4-grit to 1,200-grit. I have seen a form of wet-dry silicone paper in 3,000-grit, but anything that fine would certainly have little use in metal work in the gun shop. Up to 240-grit abrasive grains are screened for size. Grains finer than 240-grit are separated by other methods.

GRINDING WHEEL

The grinding wheel is a self-sharpening metal removal tool. Each grain, before use, has numerous sharp points or edges that act as cutting tools. These grains cut into the work being ground until they become dull. When too dull to do any more cutting, the pressure of the workpiece will cause the dull portion of the grain to break away, exposing a new sharp edge. This procedure continues until the grain is of no further use in the cutting process, and then it is released from the wheel, exposing a new, sharp grain. The bond holding abrasive grains together is the agent that releases the grains when they are too worn to cut efficiently.

Because every aspect of the manufacture of the abrasive can be controlled, the point at which the grain fractures and exposes a new cutting edge can be controlled for various operations. Aluminum oxide grains can be produced in various degrees of toughness: friable, semifriable, tough, and extra-tough. The friable grains fracture under light pressure and result in a cool cutting action. This grade is a white, almost pure aluminum oxide. "White" wheels are extensively used in toolroom grinding. Semifriable is somewhat tougher than friable and requires more pressure to break. This grain finds use in grinding softer metals. The tough and extra-tough require far more pressure to fracture the grain. These grades find use in abrasive belts, snagging operations in foundries, and steel mills.

There are six kinds of bond that hold the abrasive grains together in a wheel. The one that will concern us most is vitrified bond. Better than half of the grinding wheels manufactured today are of the vitrified bond. The bonding material is feldspar and clay. Simply put, the bond in a moist state is mixed with the abrasive, molded under high pressure, then fired in a kiln. After firing, the wheels are trimmed to their finished dimensions.

The grade of a wheel is the degree of strength with which the bonding agent holds the abrasive grains. Combined with the degree of toughness of the abrasive grains, it is an indication of the overall resistance the grains have in fracturing and being released from the wheel when too dull to cut efficiently. The grade of a wheel will vary from soft to hard.

Some means must be provided for chip clearance as the abrasive grains cut into the work. Otherwise, the face of the wheel will become clogged with chips and lose its cutting efficiency. The structure of the wheel determines the chip clearance. Basically, this is the relationship of the abrasive grains to the bond, to small open spaces or voids, uniformly dispersed throughout the wheel. These voids are instrumental in providing a rapid means of removing chips from the wheel face. Structure varies from dense to open.

Because of the wide variety of wheels available on the market, a standard method of designating grinding wheels was developed. Refer to figure 19. Column one designates the type of abrasive; column two, the grit size; column three, the grade; column four, the structure; and column five, the bond. There is a column six, but this is usually the manufacturer's private marking. As an example, AA–46–H–8–V would be a white aluminum oxide, 46-grit, medium soft grade, medium open structure, of vitrified bond.

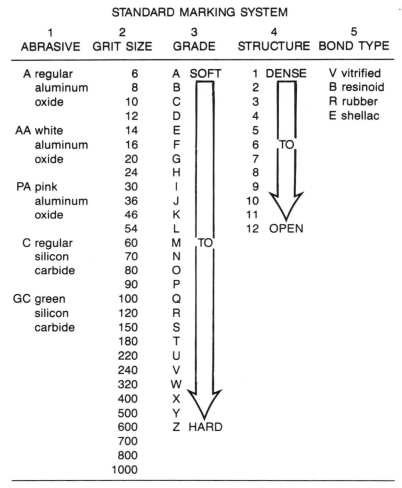

STANDARD MARKING SYSTEM

1 ABRASIVE	2 GRIT SIZE	3 GRADE	4 STRUCTURE	5 BOND TYPE
A regular	6	A SOFT	1 DENSE	V vitrified
aluminum	8	B	2	B resinoid
oxide	10	C	3	R rubber
	12	D	4	E shellac
AA white	14	E	5	
aluminum	16	F	6 TO	
oxide	20	G	7	
	24	H	8	
PA pink	30	I	9	
aluminum	36	J	10	
oxide	46	K	11	
	54	L	12 OPEN	
C regular	60	M TO		
silicon	70	N		
carbide	80	O		
	90	P		
GC green	100	Q		
silicon	120	R		
carbide	150	S		
	180	T		
	220	U		
	240	V		
	320	W		
	400	X		
	500	Y		
	600	Z HARD		
	700			
	800			
	1000			

Figure 19. The standard marking system precisely identifies a grinding wheel's construction.

There was a time when an electric grinder was considered a luxury. Not anymore. It is now possible to obtain a serviceable ½-horse-power, double-ended grinder, with wheels, for around $50. The development of grinding and abrasives has transcended the gap from limited high-tech to everyday household usage. Many basement and garage workshops are equipped with this tool. It can be used for such ordinary household tasks as sharpening scissors, kitchen knives, the kids' skates, the lawnmower blade, or for more exotic ventures, such as sharpening the amateur gunsmith's twist drills and chisels, hogging metal from various gun projects, and anything else the imagination can conjure. This is one power tool I feel no household should be without. For the purposes listed above, the grinder should be at least ⅓ horsepower, preferably ½ horsepower. Anything less than ⅓ horsepower is useless. The wheels will be between 6 inches in diameter by ½ inch wide and 7 inches by 1 inch. Since most grinding as described above will be on high-tensile-strength steel such as carbon steel and various alloy steels, the wheels should be aluminum oxide. Grit size for the coarse wheel should be 36-grit, and for the fine wheel, 60-grit. Grade and structure should be medium, with a vitrified bond. As indicated in figure 19, the coarse wheel would be identified as A–36–M–7–V and the fine wheel as A–60–L–7–V.

A few words on safety precautions are in order. The village where I grew up and now reside was famous as a cutlery manufacturing center back in the 1870s through the early 1900s. A book depicting the history of the area reprints local newspaper articles describing in gory detail accidents involving cutlery grinders. It appears that those old wheels had a habit of occasionally disintegrating while in use. These widow-makers, as they were not-so-affectionately called, would then send large chunks through the anatomy of anyone standing in the way. Though the modern grinding wheel is a far cry from these old killers, under the right conditions and abuse it too will disintegrate. I've seen it happen.

Never:
- Exceed the maxim rpm (revolutions per minute) indicated on the wheel.
- Mount a wheel on the grinder without the proper mounting flanges.
- Mount a wheel on the grinder with the improper hole size.
- Operate a grinder that has a wheel or wheels out of balance or out of round.
- Use a wheel suspected of being cracked.
- Excessively tighten the nut holding the flanges against the wheel.
- Stand directly in front of the wheel while it is turning.

Always:
- Wait about a minute after starting up a grinder before using it.
- Wear safety glasses.
- Use proper wheel guards.

Although the modern grinding wheel is self-sharpening, there are limits to this capability, and eventually the surface will become glazed with imbedded particles and dull abrasive grains that have not been released. At this stage its cutting efficiency is greatly reduced, and further use will result in little metal removal and generate excessive heat in the workpiece. When this occurs, it is necessary to dress the wheel. The dressing operation removes the clogging particles and the dull, expended abrasive grains from the surface of the wheel, exposing a clean surface with sharp, new abrasive grains. Although there are several kinds of dressers and methods of use, the most appropriate and common type for a bench grinder is the hand-held star dresser. This tool is made up of several star-shaped disks loosely mounted on a pin with solid disk spaces. The assembly is mounted in a holder with a handle (figure 20). The base of the holder rests firmly on the tool rest of the grinder, and the stars are brought against the face of the wheel,

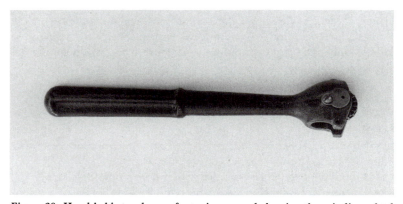

Figure 20. Hand-held star dresser for truing up and cleaning the grinding wheel face. The hooks at the bottom of the head are placed over the grinder steady rest, and the star wheels are brought up against the face of the wheel and slid across it. Sufficient pressure should be exerted against the wheel so that no sparking occurs during contact.

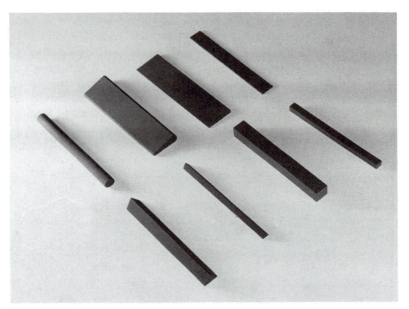

Figure 21. India slips are aluminum oxide stones in various shapes. *Top row, left to right:* round, round edge, knife, flat. *Bottom row, left to right:* large triangular, small triangular, large square, small square.

moving slowly across the face. The wheel penetration is usually several thousandths of an inch. The result is a clean, trued-up face.

SHARPENING STONES AND ABRASIVE STICKS

Grains of silicon carbide or aluminum oxide are mixed with a bonding agent and molded into various shapes. One of the more common shapes is a flat rectangle in various sizes commonly referred to as a hone, oil stone, or sharpening stone. Other shapes are shown in figure 21. These shapes are called abrasive sticks or abrasive files. Sticks and stones find much use in the gunsmith shop or any machine shop. They are available in grit ranges of coarse, medium, and fine. The most familiar flat oil stone is a combination stone with one face either coarse or medium grit, and the other face fine grit.

Though it is obvious that a coarse grit stone will cut faster than finer grits of the same type abrasive, this is not the lone criterion for determining which stone to select for a particular job. The sharpness of the abrasive determines the cutting rate. Silicon carbide grains are sharper than aluminum oxide; therefore this is the abrasive stone to use when looking for a fast cut. On the other hand, if it is more important to retain the shape of the stone, or sharp edges and contours, use aluminum oxide. Aluminum oxide grains are much tougher than silicon carbide, and the stone or stick will hold up better under heavy use. Both silicon carbide and aluminum oxide stones and sticks are suitable for use on high-tensile-strength metals. This appears to be in contradiction of earlier statements recommending aluminum oxide only for this class of metals. The reason for this is that silicon carbide grains are much more brittle than aluminum oxide. On power-grinding operations, much more pressure is involved between the work and the wheel than in hand honing, polishing, or lapping. The rate of breakdown of a silicon carbide wheel in a power operation would usually be unacceptable, though for hand operations, it is acceptable. In most applications, both silicon carbide and aluminum oxide are acceptable, because the amount of metal removal is small and the operation is in the final finishing stage. Even with the use of honing machines, a maximum of about 0.01 inch is removed from a bored hole. With hand-honing, the amount is less. Why bother then? Because the honing operation produces a uniform, smooth surface that permits mating, moving parts to move over each other with a smoothness comparable to two flat sheets of glass sliding over each other, with a thin film of oil between them. Additionally, a properly honed or stoned cutting tool is the difference between fairly sharp and really sharp.

HONING

As with any tool, there is a right and a wrong way to use a stone or stick. Unfortunately, more users of abrasive stones have adopted the wrong way. We have all seen at one time or another someone pick up a stone, spit on it, and then apply his knife, chisel, or other tool to be sharpened, and rub it in a circular motion, parallel to the surface. About all this exercise accomplishes is to further dull the cutting edge and wear a concave spot on the stone where the action is taking place. Proper hand-honing or stoning is a slow, deliberate, controlled action. Assume that you wish to stone a fairly straight cutting edge such as a jackknife blade. Start on the coarse side of the stone. Imagine that a postage stamp has been affixed to the surface of the stone, and that you wish to scrape it off without mutilating it. We'll also assume that the knife already has the proper angle of bevel ground for the cutting edge. Set the blade on the stone with the cutting edge facing the imaginary postage stamp so the full surface of the bevel is in contact with the stone. Advance the blade in a straight line, using moderate pressure and stroke speed, toward the imaginary postage stamp as though you were going to scrape it off intact in one stroke. When the end of the stroke is reached, remove the blade from the stone, lifting the cutting edge first. This is very important. If the back edge of the blade is lifted first, it is almost a certainty that the cutting edge will roll over the stone while still in contact. The result will be to blunt it. The procedure is carried out for the reverse side of the blade, still trying to scrape off the imaginary stamp. Repeat as above for both sides of the blade until a feather edge appears on the cutting edge. At this time, switch to the fine stone, using the exact procedures as with the coarse stone. When the feather edge is honed off, your cutting edge should be razor-sharp.

It is important in hand honing or stoning that the work being honed is not rocked. It must always proceed over the stone in the exact same position that it started. Additionally, all repeat strokes must begin at the same angle to the stone as the preceding strokes. This is quite easy to check after a few strokes. In the case of the knife blade, sight along the cutting edge. The bevel on each side must be straight and flat. If it is round (the roundness will be convex), then you are rocking the blade or not beginning your succeeding strokes at the same angle, or both. Always use a honing oil; a small can is inexpensive. The oil enhances the cutting action by keeping the surface of the stone clear and preventing metal particles from clogging the pores.

Abrasive sticks or files are convenient for use on items that cannot readily be worked by the flat, rectangular stone described above because of the wide variety of shapes and sizes in which they are available. They can be used for sharpening auger bits, wood gouges, reamer flutes, and numerous other cutting edges requiring special consideration. Cleaning up square or round holes or obtaining sharp internal corners becomes a simple job when the right stick is used. In pure gunsmithing applications, these sticks can be used in smoothing trigger pulls and action work in general. Abrasive sticks or files are used in the same way regular needle files and rifflers are used, as described in the previous chapter. Unlike the metal file, the abrasive stick cuts in both directions. However, it should be worked like the metal file, in one direction only. This ensures more positive control of the stroke and lessens the tendency to rock the stick.

Sticks or stones eventually become saturated with oil and the surfaces will become clogged with dirt and metal chips. When this condition is reached, they can be rejuvenated by heating. Put the stick or stone in a pan and heat it in an oven or on top of a burner. (The stone should be in a pan because a surprising amount of oil will be released.) As the stone heats up, oil will escape from the interior, opening up pores and cleaning out the dirt. Wipe the stone clean while it is still hot; otherwise, any oil in contact with it will be sucked up as it cools. A word of caution: If the kitchen stove or oven is used, make sure there is plenty of ventilation, because a considerable amount of foul-smelling smoke will be generated.

LAPPING

Lapping is a metal-removal procedure employed as a final operation in obtaining a super-accurate, super-smooth finish. As a rule, only minute high spots and surface irregularities are removed. The operation removes anywhere from 0.0002 to 0.0005 of an inch from an already accurately finished workpiece. Lapping can be performed on either flat surfaces or round surfaces, internally and externally. The lap is made from a metal softer than the metal being lapped, such as cast iron, lead, brass, or copper. A lap for lapping flat surfaces is just that: flat. For lapping holes, the lap would be a round cylinder of slightly less diameter than the hole being lapped and usually split and on an expanding mandrel. For an outside round surface, it would be a hole of slightly larger diameter than the cylinder to be lapped and split so that it could be tightened as the operation proceeds. The above are simple laps employed in hand lapping. The lap is charged with abrasive grains and a lubricant vehicle. (Charging a lap means that the abrasive grains are actually imbedded in the lap.) The operation can be conducted either by hand or machine. Machine lapping is used in production operations. Hand lapping is still used in toolrooms and model shops to produce prototypes. In custom gunsmithing work, hand lapping as described above is used to polish out rifle barrel chambers, shotgun bores and chokes, and rifle bores.

Another form of lapping does not employ the laps described above. Actually, it is close to being a combination of hand honing and hand lapping and is sometimes referred to as running in. A petroleum-based emulsion of either aluminum oxide or silicon carbide grains is thinly spread between the surfaces of mating parts, and the parts are worked in motion in the manner in which they would normally operate. If the parts are of similar hardness or similar metal, the abrasive grains will not imbed in either surface and will act as a cutting agent on both surfaces. If properly done, only high spots and impeding surface irregularities will be removed. The result will be a smoother operating mechanism with relatively little metal removed. These compounds in the ready-mixed stage are relatively inexpensive and available from Brownells, of Montezuma, Iowa, in a variety of grits.

COATED ABRASIVES

Coated abrasives are manufactured by applying loose abrasive grains to an adhesive-coated backing of cloth, paper, or fiber. The layman knows them best as sandpaper, emery paper, wet-dry sandpaper, garnet paper, or cabinet paper. Aluminum oxide cloth or paper and silicon carbide wet-dry are the coated abrasives of most importance to the gunsmith — amateur or professional. These two abrasive cloths and papers will meet the needs of almost any operational requirement in the gunsmith shop, from metal finishing to gunstock making. Additionally, they are relatively inexpensive and available at any hardware store or auto parts supply store. In short, they are the best bargain available in gunsmithing tools.

Both aluminum oxide- and silicon carbide–coated abrasives are available in 9- by 11-inch sheets, rolls of 1-inch width and up, and sanding belts of various sizes. Grits range anywhere from 36-grit to 1,200-grit. Both aluminum oxide and silicon carbide are available with a waterproof backing, which permits them to be used both wet and dry.

Coated abrasives find a multitude of uses in gunsmithing. Contrary to the average layman's notion that they are just sandpaper and suitable only for light smoothing and polishing operations, silicon carbide– and aluminum oxide–coated abrasives are metal-removal tools. The coarser grits, such as 60 and 80, remove metal at a surprising rate in hand operations. They find much use in fitting parts, smoothing actions, shaping and sanding gunstocks, and final shaping and finishing of small metal parts. By using the file with the proper combination of grit, complex contours and surfaces can be generated and highly finished. They will find extensive use in all of the projects covered in future chapters.

7

Polishing the Gun in Preparation for Blueing

The most common major service performed by the average gunsmith shop is reblueing. A first-class blueing job is the quickest, most inexpensive way of imparting a conspicuous touch of class to an otherwise drab gun. Conversely, a botched polishing job in preparation for blueing is the quickest way to destroy permanently the value of an otherwise valuable firearm. To the average gun owner, blueing evokes visions of an alchemist performing secret rituals to transmute a rusty old clunker into a thing of beauty. Such is not the case. The procedure for imparting a blue-black color to the metal is a simple chemical process that can be executed by a complete amateur, carefully following instructions in his own basement, garage, or kitchen. Usually much of the equipment is already at hand, and there are numerous salts and solutions of different types readily available on the market. With the exceptions of some instant or touch-up solutions, most provide agreeable color and acceptable durability. Each brand of blueing chemical comes with its own directions for application.

Too often, the amateur thinks that the blueing will cover up pits, scratches, and gouges in the metal. The exact opposite is true. The blueing will accentuate any flaw in the metal. Pitting that is barely perceptible on the unblued metal will stick out like the proverbial sore thumb after it is blued. Without proper polishing, *no* blueing job will look decent, regardless of the type or quality of the salts or chemicals used. It can be safely estimated that 90 percent of the success of a blueing job depends on the quality of the polishing done on the metal.

With the power grinding and buffing equipment and the abrasives available today, it is possible to impart a mirrorlike finish on the rustiest old derelict in a relatively short time. This in itself does not make for a good polishing job. On the contrary, it is quite easy to achieve a mirror finish and destroy the aesthetic value of a fine firearm at the same time. Virtually all the other characteristics of a first-class polishing job are more important than a mirror finish: removing all pitting, scratches, dents, machine marks, and polish marks; retaining sharp edges and corners where they should be sharp; retaining sharp stamped lettering and engraving; avoiding the saucering of screw holes; avoiding a ripple or washboard effect on plane surfaces and barrels (that is, retaining a true surface); and retaining original contours.

POWER POLISHING VS HAND POLISHING

You will seldom find a busy commercial gunsmith shop doing hand polishing on any gun except the most expensive. It takes an experienced man up to five or six times as long to polish a gun by hand as it would using power buffers and grinders. Although the power equipment used in the average gunsmith shop is a far cry from the production machinery used by major manufacturers, it is still production machinery as far as the average shop is concerned. A few of the larger shops offer a hand-polishing service, and you'll find that the price is about five or six times as high as with the production method. Why hand polish, then? Because no combination of power buffers, grinders, and wheels and bobs used by the most experienced polisher can produce a final result the equal of hand polishing.

The power buffer-grinder is usually a double-ended motor of between ¾ and 3 horsepower, rotating at a speed of about 1,700 or 3,400 rpm. On its shafts are mounted wheels of muslin, felt, or leather, whose circumferences are covered with a rubberized aluminum oxide compound or a grease-based silicon abrasive. The wheels range in rigidity from quite soft to rather stiff. The work to be ground or buffed is hand-held and brought into contact with the edge of the wheel. We now have a combination of high speed, a lot of power, and an abrasive that cuts rapidly.

Regardless of how stiff the wheel may appear, it is still not completely rigid. Because the contact area between the wheel and work is only tangential to the wheel, it is subject to some distortion from even the lightest pressure. Additionally, the centrifugal force caused by the rotation of the wheel adds further distortion. As it passes over stamped lettering, engraving, screw holes, or sharp edges, the wheel "weeps" into the depression. The weeping, combined with rapid cutting action, causes blurred lettering and engraving, saucered screw holes, and rounded edges. Also, it is almost impossible for even the most experienced polisher to move the work along the wheel with such uniformity of pressure and speed as to get a perfect cut. This results in a rippling effect on all surfaces. The next time you look at a gun that has been reblued, examine it carefully under a strong light or in the sunlight. You'll find evidence of all the faults described above, to a degree commensurate with the skill of the polisher who did the work.

Hand polishing, on the other hand, eliminates all the above faults at the expense of speed. The rate of metal removal is slow and closely controlled. Whereas pitting would most often be ground out with power equipment, in hand polishing it would be draw filed. The former leaves a ripple effect, and the latter, a true surface. Abrasive paper or cloth permits a greater area of contact between the metal and the cutting surface than the tangent of a wheel. Because it moves more slowly over the work, it gives the effect of greater rigidity than a fast-spinning wheel subject to centrifugal force and other distortive forces. It is sufficiently flexible for curved surfaces, yet it will not weep into the minor depressions.

Hand polishing is basically simple work requiring a minimum of experience and equipment and a maximum of perseverance and attention to detail. As a matter of fact, less experience is required to produce a superior polishing job by hand than to produce an average job with power equipment. A complete novice conscientiously following instructions should be able to give a first-class polish to an average bolt action rifle in about twelve hours.

The example gun chosen for illustrative purposes is a Japanese

7.7mm Arisaki. Like most older military rifles, it is a strong, reliable, accurate shooter. More than most, it is crudely finished. I wouldn't spend the money necessary to have any military rifle extensively customized by a professional. It would be cheaper to buy a quality commercial product. But almost any military rifle is more than worthy of the couple of bucks and the time and effort if you do the work yourself.

PREPARATION

The first step is to disassemble the gun completely, down to the last screw. The only two items remaining intact are the receiver and barrel. Separate the parts into two groups. One group will consist of all parts and screws visible when the gun is assembled; the other group is whatever is left over (figure 22).

Put the leftover parts in a suitable container, put the container away where it won't get lost, and forget about it for a while. Check the items to be blued to ensure that there are no aluminum alloy parts present. (Aluminum alloy cannot be colored by the same process used to blue ferrous metal parts.) This can easily be determined with a toy mag-

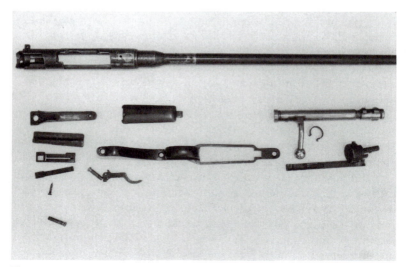

Figure 22. The stripped-down Arisaki. These are the parts to be polished, the visible parts.

net. If the magnet sticks to the metal, polish the part. If it doesn't stick, put that particular part with the parts not to be blued.

It is now necessary to remove all the remaining old finish from the metal. This can be done with a commercial rust and blue remover, or you can mix your own. One part hydrochloric acid to six parts water makes an excellent solution. But before applying the blue remover, the metal must be free of all grease, oil, and dirt. Wash it down with an appropriate solvent, such as gasoline. After the blueing remover solution has been applied, scrub all the metal with No. 00 steel wool and kitchen scouring powder, then rinse thoroughly. When it is dry, apply a light coat of oil to prevent rusting. The clean, deblued, scrubbed metal will have a frosty, grayish appearance. All pits, scratches, and rusted areas will be clearly visible. Take all the cleaned metal parts out into the bright sunlight and examine them carefully, so that you know precisely where the blemishes in the metal are.

DRAW FILING

Almost any gun in need of reblueing will have pitting to some degree. Although it is possible to remove the pitting by sanding, the time and effort involved are usually excessive. Draw filing is almost always in order as the first step in the polishing process. Using a heavily padded vise to prevent damage to the gun, secure the receiver in the vise. Care must be taken not to clamp down too hard and damage the receiver. With a 10-inch mill bastard file, draw file the entire length of the barrel over the areas where pits and scratches are in evidence. Be careful not to remove too much metal over stamped lettering. It is quite easy to work right up to most lettering. Continue rotating the gun in the vise, and draw file the barrel until you have covered the entire surface and removed all blemishes. When you are satisfied that all pits and scratches have been removed, take the gun out in the bright sunlight and examine the draw-filed surface under a magnifying glass for any minute pitting you may have missed. This pitting will give the appearance of tiny black specks and may be difficult to see. (You can be sure that it won't be difficult to see on the finished blued gun.) If you discover any, mark them with a red crayon and draw file them out. Once you are satisfied that all blemishes have been removed, return the gun to the vise — this time with the barrel secured in the vise.

Most receivers are configured so that they can be draw filed lengthwise. Certain ones with a contoured bridge, such as the 98 Mauser, will require a straight filing in that area. For this purpose, a 6-inch half-round bastard works nicely. Draw file lengthwise where possible, and cross file where necessary. Repeat the inspection under bright sunlight.

POLISHING

Six grits of aluminum oxide or silicon carbide cloth or paper are used in the polishing phase: 80, 120, 240, 320, 400, and 500. Three sheets of each should be sufficient. (I like the open coat production paper best, although any type of backing works well.)

CROSS POLISHING

Secure the receiver in the padded vise. With a pair of old scissors, cut a strip of 80-grit paper about 1-inch wide (cut the paper the long way) and polish as indicated in figure 23. Your first few strokes will

Figure 23. Cross polishing. The motions of the abrasive cloth or paper against the barrel are exactly the same as those used with a shoe-shine rag.

reveal that the barrel is not truly round but a series of "flats" from the draw filing. Continue this procedure over the entire length and circumference of the barrel with the 80-grit until all of the flats and file marks disappear and the barrel looks as though it had been turned down in a lathe. Don't hesitate to change the abrasive paper or cloth when it becomes dull or filled. It is false economy to continue with worn-out paper. Make a special point of ensuring that the sanding goes all the way back to the receiver and all the way forward to the muzzle. For some reason, these two areas seem to be focal points when people are looking at the finished product, yet they tend to be ignored when people are working on them. At this point it is necessary to emphasize the necessity to *remove completely* all marks from the immediately preceding operation. If you don't, you'll never get them in the later polishing steps.

DRAW POLISHING

Draw polishing is done in a direction parallel to the axis of the barrel (figure 24) in a manner similar to draw filing. Cut a 1½-inch strip of 120-grit paper and fold as indicated in figure 25. With the open edges in the direction of the axis of the barrel, commence polishing the barrel lengthwise. Continue the polishing until all cross polishing marks are removed. Since it will be nearly impossible to draw polish the barrel flush up to the receiver, finish that portion within ½ inch of the receiver by cross polishing.

The above procedures are repeated, using successively finer grit until the final draw is completed with the 500-grit. The proper sequence is to cross polish with 80-grit; draw polish with 120-grit; cross polish with 240-grit; draw polish with 320-grit; cross polish with 400-grit; and draw polish with 500-grit. Once again, ensure that all polishing marks from the previous polishing are removed before proceeding to the next-finer grade of paper or cloth.

Most receivers lend themselves better to cross polishing all the way because of their configuration and the shell port cutout. About 95 percent of the receiver can be easily cross polished in the manner indicated in figure 23. A few areas, such as the thumb cutout for clip loading on military receivers and the small radius on the forward left-hand side of the shell port, require a little improvising. The abrasive paper or cloth can be wrapped around a dowel of suitable diameter and used as a file. I use either my thumb or my little finger instead

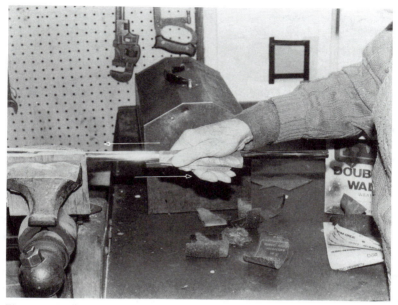

Figure 24. Draw polishing. The cloth or paper is slid back and forth in a direction parallel to the axis of the bore.

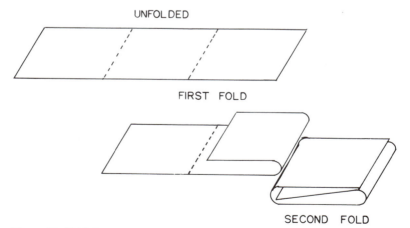

UNFOLDED

FIRST FOLD

SECOND FOLD

Figure 25. Fold the abrasive paper or cloth for draw polishing and remove the marks left by cross polishing.

of a wooden dowel. They conform to most radii . . . but they are calloused.

SMALL PARTS

Everything that is left to be polished after the barrel and action falls into this category. The trigger guard is easily draw filed lengthwise all the way. The outside curved surfaces (convex) are easily draw filed with a 6-inch triangular file. The inside radii of the guard loop can be draw filed with a 6-inch half-round bastard. The radii just forward and rear of the guard loop are well adapted to an oval needle file. I've seldom seen a trigger guard that needed or was adapted to straight or cross filing. All polishing with abrasive paper should be draw polishing.

Often screw slots become badly damaged through repeated use of improper screwdrivers or in a semisuccessful attempt to remove a frozen screw. As long as a portion of the head has not been broken or chewed off, they can easily be repaired. Secure the screw body in the vise with the bottom of the head resting on top of the vise jaws. With a 4-ounce machinists' hammer, lightly pound the deformed portion of the head back into its original shape. After this has been done, secure

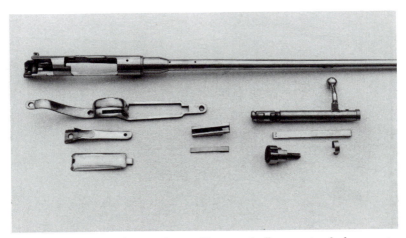

Figure 26. The polished gun and parts. No power buffers ever touched any part. All corners, edges, and contours are intact, and there are no visible machine or polishing marks.

the screw body in a electric hand drill. With the drill held in the vise, run a 10-inch second cut mill file lightly over the top of the rotating screw head. Remove only enough metal to eliminate all blemishes. Polish the head with the various grits of abrasive paper while it is still rotating in the drill. After the head has been polished, return the screw to the vise, and recut the slot with a 6-inch knife file. It should be as good as new.

If you have done your work carefully, the final result should look like figure 26. The total time required for this particular gun was 5 hours and 47 minutes. Remember, to begin with, this gun was very crudely finished.

8

Blueing the Gun

The main purpose of coloring the metal on a gun is to impart a dull finish to the shiny metal so that the metal will not reflect light and distract the shooter or frighten game. A very close second reason is to make the gun attractive. Contrary to popular belief, blueing accomplishes little in the way of rust prevention. It is, in fact, an induced, controlled rusting.

The practice of coloring gun metal dates back at least to the seventeenth century. It originally acquired the name *browning*, because the resultant color was brown. Sometime in the 1800s, a sharp gunsmith discovered that by altering the chemical composition of the solution and the process, he could get a blue-black finish. The term *browning* continued to be used, despite the final color, even to the mid-twentieth century. In recent years, we've settled on calling the process blueing for a blue color and browning for a brown color.

A few of the many methods of coloring steel are acid, caustic, carbon, carbon vapor, heat, plating, and Parkerizing. Additionally, an almost infinite number of variations and formulas can be applied to each. It appears that in years past, almost every gunsmith of consequence had his own jealously guarded secret formula. R. H. Angier, in his book *Firearm Blueing and Browning*, lists some 230 formulas. I would guess that this is only a small fraction of those available.

For the tinkerer with at least a high school chemistry background, it's fun and satisfying to mix up a few batches of your own. If you're so inclined, I highly recommend Angier as the source for almost any kind of blueing formula. If you'd rather omit this exercise, almost any type of solution is readily available through gunsmith supply houses. Brownells of Montezuma, Iowa, carries nearly the complete spectrum. A word of advice: you'll not save money by mixing your own. Chemicals purchased in small amounts at the local druggist cost an arm and a leg. For this reason, no formulas for solutions will be given in this book. Within each specific category all solutions are basically similar, and their application and usage are the same.

BLUEING EQUIPMENT

The blueing procedures described in this chapter all require the same basic equipment: a source of heat, containers to hold the various parts, wire hooks to suspend certain parts in the container, and small wire baskets to hold the smaller parts.

Most of this equipment is already available in the average home. I began my blueing career using my mother's kitchen stove as a source of heat. The tank that contained the barrel and action was made from iron stove pipe (figure 27), and the smaller parts were processed in cooking pots. As a matter of fact, a 10-inch stainless steel pot is all the container necessary for the average handgun. Wire baskets to hold small parts, such as screws, were fashioned from ordinary kitchen strainers; wire hooks were made from wire coat hangers. When the weather wasn't humid enough to induce natural rusting for a particular process, I would run about 2 inches of water into the bathtub, hang the parts in the bathroom, and shut the door.

Such equipment and facilities may sound primitive and basic, but I assure the reader that they produced many first-class blueing jobs with little more trouble than the more sophisticated equipment I later acquired. (A word of caution: since the tank has the end pieces soldered on, *never* use it for the caustic hot dip process. The solution will rapidly destroy the solder and you'll find it all over the kitchen.) The main problem with using the kitchen and the daily cooking utensils is that eventually someone else in the house may lose patience and throw

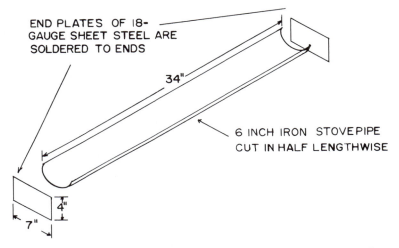

END PLATES OF 18-GAUGE SHEET STEEL ARE SOLDERED TO ENDS

34"

6 INCH IRON STOVEPIPE CUT IN HALF LENGTHWISE

4"

7"

Figure 27. Homemade stove-top blueing tank. Its practical use is limited only to the cold rust process, but it does work, and it's useful.

out the whole mess. Additionally, there is a natural tendency to want better equipment as one gains experience.

An excellent stove frame can be made from ordinary angle iron. Figure 28 illustrates the frame for a two-burner, two-tank stove made from 1 by 1 by ⅛-inch angle iron, with the legs made from 1½ by 1½ by ⅛-inch angle iron. Although these angle iron sizes provide sufficient rigidity and light weight, there is nothing sacred about their size. Almost any size within reason that you can pick up at a decent price from your local scrap metal dealer will work just as well. Old mattress or bed frames would work nicely. Construction can be either bolted or welded. The "double clothesline pole" structures on both ends of the frame are used to support rods from which the barreled action and other parts are suspended by hangers for immersion in the tanks.

Two heating units are attached to the underside of the frame (not shown in figure 28). Each is centrally positioned under its tank support space. Natural or LP gas burners or electric strip heating elements may be used. I don't recommend electric heating, which has several disadvantages:

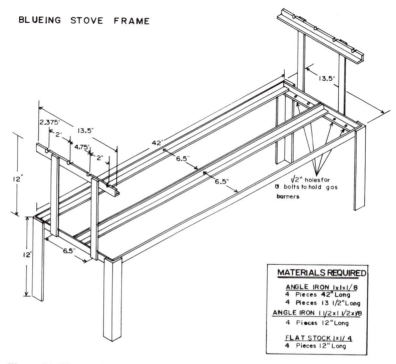

Figure 28. Two-tank blueing stove frame. Construction can be either welded or bolted.

- The initial cost is higher.
- The operational cost is higher.
- The bottom side of the element must be thermally insulated with a refractory material, or half the heat will be lost to the atmosphere.
- The average home isn't wired to provide the power required.
- It takes longer to heat the tanks to the required temperature.

Of the two gases, natural and LP, I prefer LP gas simply because the rig is more mobile and the hookup is much more convenient. A 25-pound tank of LP gas will last a long time.

Gas burners can be either made or bought. The local gas company can supply the technical information on hole size and spacing, pipe size, orifice size, and cap size. Years ago I made the rig in figure 29, including the burners. Shortly after its completion, I discovered that I could have purchased the burners complete for about the same cost of making them. If you can buy a tool that's already in production, don't bother making it.

The typical pipe burner is about 1½ to 1¾ inches outside diameter and 48 to 50 inches long (including the orifice and cap) and has a capacity of 40,000 to 45,000 Btu. A burner of this capacity will rapidly heat the contents of a 6 by 6 by 40-inch tank to any temperature the average home craftsman or small gunsmith shop will use in various types of blueing.

The tanks for use with the stove in figure 28 would be 6 by 6 by 40-inches. These tanks should be of black iron with welded construction. Make sure that the tanks are welded. The brass in brazed seams would eventually poison a caustic hot dip solution. Soldered seams would be rapidly eaten away by the hot dip salts. As with the stove

Figure 29. The author's homemade, semiprofessional, mobile blueing rig from a long-past era. If it was too hot in the garage, I'd just move it out onto the driveway. Many a gun was blued in this outfit before I acquired more sophisticated equipment; I still use it for my own occasional jobs.

burners, you'd be better off getting ready-made tanks from a gun-smithing supply house than trying to make them yourself or having the local sheet-metal man make them.

Hooks for suspending the barreled action and larger parts in the tanks can be made from 3/16-inch cold roll steel. Figure 30 gives some suggested shapes. Ordinary kitchen strainers will hold small parts; just make sure they are not made of aluminum. Usually strainers made with an iron mesh have a coating of tin. This tin coating must be removed by dipping the strainer in a solution of one part sulfuric acid and six parts of water. If you wish to make your own, both stainless steel and black iron screen are available from gunsmith supply houses.

DEGREASING

Before we embark on the actual mechanics of blueing, two very important items must be stressed: the metal must be *absolutely free* of all

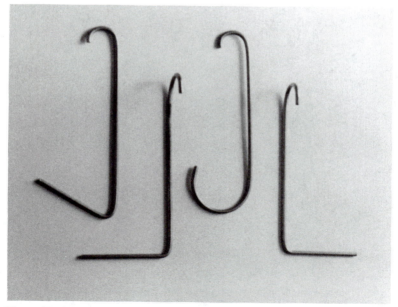

Figure 30. An assortment of part holders made from 3/16-inch cold roll. For the occasional job, coat hangers bent in a similar fashion can substitute nicely.

grease, oil, and foreign matter; and once the blueing procedure starts, *do not touch* any part to be blued with your hands or with anything that could transfer foreign matter, or you'll have to start the procedure over. This degreasing procedure applies to all the different blueing processes.

Wash down all parts to be blued with a solvent to remove the bulk of grease, dirt, polish, and other residue. In the absence of anything else, gasoline will do. Use an old toothbrush to get inside the action and other nooks and crannies. Any hidden lump of grease or residue carried over to the blueing process could contaminate the bath and botch the job. When the parts have been thoroughly washed, remove any trace of the solvent. At this point, the parts will be immersed in a boiling degreasing solution.

Many of the old-time gunsmiths advocated inserting wooden plugs into both ends of the barrel before immersing them in the degreasing solution and blueing, the rationale being that this would protect the bore. I've never seen any degreaser or commonly used blueing solution that would harm a bore. On the contrary, there is an overwhelming reason *not* to plug the bore. The heat of the bath will cause the air in the barrel to expand, and there is always the strong possibility that this could pop the plugs. I know of several instances when this happened. In one such instance, the gunsmith was unfortunate enough to be close to the blueing tank and received a hot spray of blueing salts on his face. His glasses undoubtedly saved his eyes.

There are several commercial degreasers advertised specifically for the gunsmith. Undoubtedly they're good, but probably no better than products already available in the average kitchen. Ordinary household lye (sodium hydroxide) is as good as any. I've even had excellent results with automatic dishwasher detergent. Just don't use a sudsy laundry detergent or you'll find yourself engulfed in a mountain of suds.

Fill both tanks with water to a depth of about 4 inches, and bring it to a boil. To one of the tanks add 4 to 5 tablespoons of lye (or whatever degreaser you are using) per gallon of water. When the degreaser has dissolved in the water, insert the parts and boil for fifteen minutes. After fifteen minutes in the degreaser, *immediately* transfer the parts into the tank with plain water. Let the parts remain in the plain boiling water for two minutes, then remove them and hang them up to dry. At this point your hand must *not* touch any portion that must be blued. Handle all parts with either the attached hook or clean paper towels.

Assuming that the tap water in your area does not have an unusually high mineral content, the next step is the blueing process. If you do have hard water, some discoloration might appear on the metal, and one more step is necessary. Handling all metal parts with clean paper towels, thoroughly scour them with a clean pad of No. 00 steel wool and kitchen scouring powder. Rinse thoroughly under a faucet with hot water and hang to dry. The discoloration should now be gone and your gun ready for blueing. Caution: don't delay the blueing process, or the parts will begin to rust.

COLD RUSTING PROCESS

Quite often when the term *cold rusting* is used in reference to blueing, the novice will assume instant cold blueing. Nothing could be further from the truth. The cold rusting process is slow, sometimes taking seven to ten days to complete. This is the original method used to brown iron or steel. Through advances in chemistry and other refinements, it evolved into the acid rust blue used in modern times. Common until World War II, it is seldom used today except on the highest quality, most expensive rifles and shotguns. The process simply does not lend itself to modern, fast-production methods. The color it produces is a soft, subdued blue-black. Once you have seen a cold rust blued gun, no other type of finish will ever seem satisfactory. For durability it can't be beat, resisting wear better than any other type of blueing. An additional plus for this King of Blues is that it lends itself so readily to home usage.

After degreasing, when the parts are cool and dry, take a cotton ball with a pair of degreased needle nose pliers and saturate it with the cold blueing solution. Squeeze out the excess solution. With long, even strokes and moderate pressure, swab the solution over all areas to be blued. Only enough solution should be applied to the metal to wet it. If any runs or drips occur, too much is being used. The metal will turn a light, dull gray immediately. If the blueing didn't "take" any place, shiny metal will be exposed. This means either that degreasing was incomplete, the spot was touched or brushed by something oily, or the spot was missed in the initial application of blueing. Run the swab over the shiny area. If it takes, good. If it doesn't take, go back to square one and repeat the whole degreasing and blueing process up to where you left off. After all areas have been covered, hang the parts in a damp, humid place to rust. Humidity is a necessity for this process. Without rust, there will be no blue, and without humidity, there will be no rust. If it's fall or winter and the atmosphere is dry, try the bathroom routine. Fill the tub with 2 inches of water, hang the parts, and shut the door.

Usually, after twelve to twenty-four hours, all parts will become covered with a coat of red rust. At this time, they are returned to a tank with clean water and boiled for fifteen minutes. After boiling, the parts are hung up to dry and cool. While they are still hot, blow away accumulated water droplets in contours and screw holes. When the parts are cool, using a new, clean, No. 00 steel wool pad, thoroughly remove all the oxide covering from all parts. This is called carding. The purpose of boiling is to kill the action of the blueing solution and loosen the oxide covering. You'll find that it comes off easily.

Your first pass, after carding, may produce any color from a dull gray to a light blue; it may be splotched, or it may be uniform. Many old-timers insisted that if the first application were not perfectly uniform, it would be necessary either to repeat the whole procedure from the beginning or to make a deal with the devil. Nonsense! Each succeeding pass will deepen the color and make it more uniform. When all parts have been thoroughly carded with steel wool, repeat the application of the blueing solution, rusting, boiling, and steel wool carding as before.

Depending on the hardness of the metal, anywhere from three to eight passes as described above will be necessary before the desired depth and uniformity of color are achieved. After you have reached the depth of color you desire, give all parts one more carding with a steel wool pad saturated with oil. When this procedure is completed, thoroughly wipe out the inside of the barrel and all outside surfaces. Wipe down all parts with a good grade of gun or machine oil or one of the polarized oils made for after-gun-blueing.

When your job is completed, you will agree that it was hard, meticulous work. You will also agree that it has no equal.

HOT RUSTING PROCESS

This method is often called the quick method. A complete gun can be blued in one to two hours. It is not a very relaxing couple of hours, however. Over the years I've become convinced that the gunsmith utilizing this method must have the speed, coordination, and physical conditioning of a lightweight boxer. Fast moves and quick work are mandatory.

The hot rusting process is capable of producing a superb blueing job when the solution is just right for the steel being blued. The result will be a soft, velvety blue of exquisite appearance. On the other hand, I've seen several shades of blue and purple on the same gun where the steel was of a different hardness or composition for different components. Often it is necessary to vary the proportions of the ingredients in the solution to match the steel being blued. Mixing your own permits some experimentation. Although this is probably the least foolproof and most difficult process of those described in this chapter, it is certainly worthwhile for the serious tinkerer to try.

In some ways the hot rusting application procedure resembles the application of the cold rust solution; in other ways, it is the opposite. The key word is *hot*. The solution should be hot and applied to the metal while hot. In both procedures the method of application is the same, a cotton swab held with needle nose pliers.

Take a small mayonnaise or similiar jar and pour in about an inch of the hot rusting solution. Make a holder out of a wire coat hanger for the jar so that it can be suspended in a tank without danger of being accidentally knocked over and spilling the blueing solution. Fill the tank with about 4 inches of water, insert the parts to be blued into the water, and suspend the container holding the blueing solution into the water. Bring the water to a boil. Leave everything in the blueing tank until you are reasonably sure that the gun parts and the blueing solution are almost the same temperature as the boiling water — about ten minutes is a pretty safe bet. Now work fast. Remove the parts to be blued one at a time. As soon as the part is dried, swab on the hot solution as you would the cold blueing solution, only much faster. The part must not be permitted to cool down while the solution is being applied. It should dry almost instantaneously, with a resulting bluish-gray color. When one part is done, remove the next part and follow the same procedure. When all parts have received an application, return them to the boiling water for two or three minutes. The action of the boiling water will induce rusting. Remove the parts and card off the rust. When all parts have been thoroughly carded, return them to the boiling water for several minutes in order to heat them again. Repeat the solution application process, rusting process, and carding, as above. With each pass, the color should deepen and become more uniform. Depending on the hardness and composition of the steel, anywhere from three to six passes may be necessary before the final depth and color are reached.

As with the cold rust process, when the final desired color has been reached, give all parts a final rubdown with an oily steel wool pad. When the rubdown is complete, wipe clean and apply a light coat of oil.

HOT DIP PROCESS

This method was originally introduced around 1901 but did not come into common use until the 1930s. It lends itself well both to the mass production of industry and to professional and amateur gunsmith use. The process is simple and quick and can be readily carried out with the equipment described in this chapter, with the addition of an accurate thermometer capable of measuring temperature to about 350°F. Almost all guns of recent manufacture are blackened by this process, and it is almost universally used by professional gunsmiths. The complete process usually requires about a half hour in the bath and about ten to fifteen minutes in a rinse tank of clean, boiling water. The color produced by the hot dip method is not blue; it is a black oxide. The degree of luster of the final finish has little to do with the chemicals used. If the steel was dull before blackening, it will be dull after. If it had a high polish, the final finish will have a high luster. The finish wears reasonably well and can be pleasing in appearance.

The above fanfare given to the ease and simplicity of the hot dip process can be somewhat misleading. Like anything else, it has its drawbacks and quirks. Certain things must *never* be introduced into the bath. Aluminum or its alloys will cause a violent reaction and ruin the bath for future use. Copper and brass will eventually poison the caustic solution and cut its useful life short, although without the violence of aluminum. The hot dip solution attacks solder. A pair of soft-soldered double barrels left in the bath for ten to fifteen minutes is just as likely to come out without ribs as with them. Even if they are still on, they are almost certain to fly off after the shotgun has been fired a few times. This tendency to attack solder can be greatly reduced by adding cyanide to the bath. I don't recommend that the home amateur use cyanide. It is the deadliest of poisons, and one small mishap could result in instant death. Cast-iron parts usually require a five- to ten-minute immersion in either a solution of six parts water to one part hydrochloric acid, or a commercial rust remover. After this immersion, they are again rinsed. Without this treatment, cast iron often takes on an ugly reddish color. Nickel steel must be blued at a temperature of 15° to 20°F higher than carbon and most alloy steels, or the resultant color may be a reddish purple.

Too low an operating temperature with carbon steel parts will result in gray rather than black. Too high an operating temperature will result in a reddish color.

Blueing salts, as they are usually called, can be purchased in quantities ranging from 40 to 400 pounds. Instructions for their use are almost always furnished. (I say *almost* always, because a couple of times I've purchased brands of salts other than those I normally use, and they arrived *sans* instructions.) Although most brands are mixed and used with the same ballpark water-to-salts ratio and operating temperatures, they should always be used in strict accordance with the manufacturer's instructions. Be certain that you get the instructions.

The usual bath mixture runs anywhere from 6 to 10 pounds of salts per gallon of water. A 6 by 6 by 40–inch tank would normally be filled to hold about 4½ gallons of solution. (In a tank of these dimensions, a 1-inch level of liquid is 1 gallon. The final solution depth in the tank would be about 4½ inches.) A ballpark figure for a solution requiring 9 pounds of salts per gallon of water would be ⅔ gallon of water per 6 pounds of salts, to produce 1 gallon of solution. In a 6 by 6 by 40–inch tank, this means approximately 3 gallons of water (3-inch depth in the tank) and 27 pounds of salts will produce 4½ gallons of solution. Once again, it must be stressed that although the above figures are close, they are still ballpark figures. Follow the manufacturer's instructions. A large amount of heat is released when the salts are initially added to the water. Therefore, add the salts slowly and mix thoroughly. Too large a quantity suddenly introduced into the water could cause the whole mess to boil over or even erupt.

A word of caution: the hot dip solution is a powerful caustic. While hot, it can cause extremely painful burns. It is a good idea to wear a protective face shield and heavy neoprene gloves, not only when mixing the solution, but also when working with it. Even the most experienced professional has at one time or another accidentally dropped an aluminum part or something else into the bath and precipitated a minor volcanic eruption. Should you get any of the solution on your skin, flush it with large quantities of water. In case of serious burns, see a doctor immediately and advise him that you have caustic burns.

Most commercial salts function between 285° and 300°F. The optimum operating temperature is also the temperature at which the solution boils when it is mixed in the proper proportions. As an example, if the manufacturer's instructions state that the best blueing temperature is 290°F, a proper mixture will boil at that temperature. (Here's where the thermometer is so important.) If it begins boiling at a lower temperature, the solution is too weak and either more salts must be added or some of the excess water must be boiled off. If it's only a few degrees below the prescribed temperature, the latter action is better. If the temperature rises above 290°F, more water must be added to dilute the bath. This can be a tricky function while the solution is hot. *Never* pour a large amount of water into the hot solution. You will get a reaction similar to pouring water on a hot wood stove except, in addition, you may receive a spray of hot salts. Utilizing a long-handled stainless steel dipper, add the water very slowly and very carefully in one corner until the bath temperature comes to the prescribed level and it begins to boil. When the proper temperature has been reached and the solution is at a mild boil, the upper limit of the temperature should be controlled by the addition of water, since the water in the bath will boil out. Regulation of the heat applied should be used only to control the intensity of the boil at proper operating temperatures.

Once you have mixed the salts to the proper proportions and the bath is at the recommended blueing temperatures, you are ready for blueing. Suspend the degreased barreled action or actions, and major parts in the bath, using hooks hung from the crossbar suspension system on the stove frame. Be careful that the parts are not touching the tank bottom or sides. Since the tank itself will be somewhat hotter than the bath, it would transmit its higher temperature to the parts being blued and could result in discoloration where contact is made. Smaller parts will be suspended in the iron mesh baskets in a similar manner. The blackening process usually requires from fifteen to thirty minutes in the bath to achieve the desired color and maximum penetration. Once this is reached, all parts are transferred to the second tank of boiling, clean water to remove the bath film remaining on them. It is inevitable that residual salts will work their way into nooks and crannies and between the barrel and the action where it is screwed in. After a few days, these salts will blossom out as a semisolid white powder. For the home craftsman, it's merely a matter of wiping the residue away. For the professional doing a lot of blueing, it can be embarrassing and time-consuming to have a parade of disgruntled customers returning with these unwanted decorations. There are chemicals to add to a rinse that will eliminate this tendency, and if you should decide to go into the blueing business, I strongly recommend that they be used. Brownells of Montezuma, Iowa, carries just about everything currently available in this line.

When the blueing and rinsing are completed, all parts are thoroughly wiped down, including the bore. All parts are then thoroughly coated inside and out with the water displacement oil and hung up so the excess oil will drip out.

Summary: for anyone who aspires to become a professional gunsmith, I can't think of a better way of breaking into the field than by starting a basement or garage reblueing business. The initial capital outlay is relatively small, and there is no faster way of learning the intricacies of a wide variety of guns than by continually disassembling and reassembling them. In addition, it is the fastest way of establishing a reputation as a meticulous craftsman. It has been my experience that the average hunter knows little about the mechanics of his gun. Little appreciation is ever given to the time and skill necessary to make and fit an intricate part for an obsolete gun, simply because the customer never sees it and doesn't know what's involved. A first-class blueing job, on the other hand, is almost the first thing noticed on a gun and is understood by everyone. But if your intentions are to remain an amateur, there is nothing more satisfying than looking at your favorite shotgun or rifle with pride and saying, "I did it myself."

9

Small Parts and Miscellaneous Work

From the late 1890s until after World War I, a great many inexpensive shotguns were dumped on the American market. Some were made in this country; many were made in Europe. One thing that characterized these bargains was that they were mostly junk. They were generally manufactured by fly-by-night makers for various hardware stores and carried just about any name the retailer specified. They were made of inferior materials, in poorly tooled plants, with little regard for quality control. Unfortunately, they still keep showing up in surprisingly large numbers and are easily recognized by their brand name, or lack thereof. If it doesn't bear the name of one of the reputable makers, such as Winchester, Remington, Stevens, Savage, Iver Johnson, Harrington and Richardson, L. C. Smith, Ithaca, and Le Fevre, don't mess with it. If you already own one, hang it up over the fireplace and leave it there.

On the other hand, a shotgun bearing one of the above names, in reasonably good condition except for some minor broken or missing part, could be well worth salvaging for use as a utility or back-up shotgun. Often only a new firing pin or a tightening up of the action is all that is needed. Many such guns, however, have deeply suffered the ravages of age, use, and abuse to the point of no return. This is a judgment you will have to make.

If the gun in question is a Parker, L. C. Smith, Fox Sterlingworth, A. H. Fox, or one of the English guns, such as Greener, Manton, or Westley Richards, you have the very best. These were expensive shotguns made of the best materials with meticulous care. On today's market they are worth a small fortune. It doesn't take much of a mishap while you are working on one of these to lower their value drastically. Unless you have great confidence in your abilities at this point, my advice is to use the services of the best professional gunsmith. For the time being, stick to lower-priced guns.

THE FIRING PIN

The firing pin strikes the primer on the cartridge and causes it to detonate. Replacing a broken firing pin was the most frequent of all the repairs I made. Frequently, factory replacement parts are readily available. If this is the case, definitely use a factory part. Many times, however, the gun is obsolete and no parts are available, or if available, delivery time is so long that hunting season will be over before the part arrives. In that case, making your own pin is the logical thing to do.

For the kinds of shotguns we are addressing, most firing pins are simple and lend themselves to home construction. In fact, they are so simple that too many shooters, with no knowledge of the consequences of an improper firing pin, make their own homemade firing pins for shotguns, using everything from a modified roofing nail to a piece of a knitting needle. Some protrude so far beyond the breech face that one would reasonably assume that each round fired would result in a punctured primer. Reality and luck being what they are, sometimes even the laws of physics and mechanics are overridden. Their owners swear that they have been "usin' that pin for years and it works fine." Others, however, are not so fortunate and receive a spray of gases in the face from a punctured primer.

Protrusion, tip shape, and diameter are critical in the design of a firing pin. Unless each of these is correctly determined, the final result

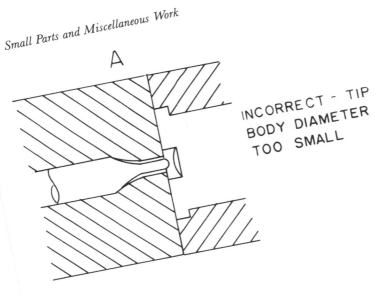

A

INCORRECT - TIP
BODY DIAMETER
TOO SMALL

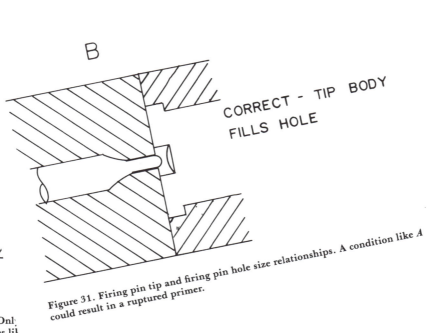

B

CORRECT - TIP BODY
FILLS HOLE

Figure 31. Firing pin tip and firing pin hole size relationships. A condition like *A* could result in a ruptured primer.

Figure 32. Only
many shapes lik

tory. With the impact force concentrated on an extremely small area, penetration of the primer would occur on impact.

Protrusion is the distance the firing pin sticks out beyond the face of the breech or bolt when it is fully extended. Assuming that the head-space is perfect (± 0) and that the base of the cartridge or primer is flush against the breech or bolt face, protrusion is the depth the firing pin would imprint into the primer. This amount is rather fixed; primer design is the determinate. Generally, between 0.055 and 0.065 inch is considered acceptable, with 0.058 inch considered optimum.

A METAL-TURNING LATHE

Logic dictates that at this point we design and construct a firing pin. But since we need a lathe to make a firing pin, we'll build a lathe first. The material necessary to construct this lather are a mandrel; ⅜- or ½-inch drill chuck that will adapt to the mandrel; a ¼ or ⅓ horsepower electric motor; suitable pulleys for the motor and man-drel; a V belt of suitable size; and a steady rest. Figure 33 illustrates the completed lathe. All that is necessary is that it be hooked up to a suitable motor. The steady rest shown came from an old wood lathe; one could just as easily be fashioned from 1-inch angle iron. If you frequent yard sales, you might pick up all of the items necessary for about $5.

This contraption is just like the first metal lathe I had when I was a teenager. Its use is limited to light cuts and small work. The cutting tools are ground from high-speed steel lathe tool bits. The shapes in no way resemble those that would be used on a conventional metal lathe; they are closer to the shapes of wood-turning chisels. The height of the steady rest depends on the size of the tool bits you will use. The rig pictured in figure 33 is set up for ⅜-inch tool bits. The steady rest height is adjusted so that when the tool bit is sitting on it, the cutting edge is at the center height of the work, or the steady rest is ⅜ inch below the center of the work. The steady rest should be as close to the work as possible and still permit the cutting tool to be seated on it solidly. The work should not revolve any faster than 800 rpm. All work being done should be worked close to the chuck, otherwise you'll experience chatter. The worked-on part of the stock that is held in the chuck should not be considered useable, because in all likelihood it will not turn out concentric with the portion being turned. The nonconcentricity is the result of inaccuracies in the

Figure 33. The basic components for a crude homemade lathe. These parts were recovered from a box of old scrap in the corner of my garage. The chuck just happened to fit the arbor shaft, so it was attached as is. If I were really going to use it other than for illustration purposes, I would rework things so that the chuck adapter would be as close as possible to the arbor frame. This would be a more rigid setup and greatly reduce chatter. A ⅓-horsepower motor will provide the necessary power.

chuck. In summary, it is used as a wood-turning lathe would be used. I know a master bamboo fly rod maker who uses a rig of the same principle. This happens to be a 9-inch South Bend Bench lathe that should have been junked years ago. About the only thing that can be said for it is that it has a chuck that turns when the power is turned on. He uses this contraption to make ferrules for fly rods; exquisite, delicate ferrules that wind up on bamboo fly rods that cost up to $2,000. His cutting tools are identical to the ones just described.

Figure 34 illustrates two of the turning tools that will be used most often. On a conventional engine lathe, a round nose tool would be used on a finish cut, and a relatively sharp pointed tool would be used for a rough cut. They would also have a back rake and a side rake ground on them. The tools shown in figures 34*A* and *B* have neither,

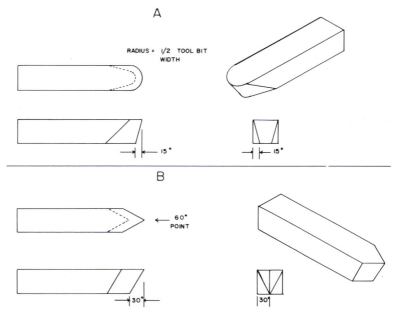

Figure 34. Turning tools for use with the lathe in figure 33. These are ground from ⁵⁄₁₆-inch or ³⁄₈-inch high-speed steel lathe tool bits. Be sure that they are securely mounted in a handle.

they have only front clearance and side clearance. In contrast to an engine lathe, the rounded nose tool of figure 34*A* would be used for diameter reduction, or rough cut, on the work. It would also be used to turn a radius up to a shoulder. The pointed tool would be used to take a finish cut on a straight piece. The appropriate side edge of the tool would be used. The point can be used to complete a sharp shoulder. The tool bits should be securely held in a handle, such as a file handle. All work is finished with a file and abrasive paper or cloth while it rotates.

FIRING PIN CONSTRUCTION

Figure 35 illustrates some of the more common firing pin shapes encountered in break-open shotguns. The pin shown in 35*A* is of the type usually found in double-barrel shotguns with side locks. It is spring-loaded, with a coil spring around the narrower body. One end of the spring rests against a shoulder in the receiver and the other end against the shoulder on the pin, so that when there is no hammer pressure on the pin, it will be fully retracted. The base of the pin (the smaller diameter) passes through a hole in a cap that screws into the receiver. This cap holds the assembly in place. Figure 35*B* is a similar pin, except for the manner in which the assembly is held in the receiver. It, too, is spring-loaded. This type is mainly found in single barrel shotguns, as are figures 35*C*, *D*, and *E*. The crosshatch areas on the pins are milled out to a depth of about half of the body diameter. A pin or screw passing through the thickness of the receiver also passes through the milled-out area of the firing pin. This pin or screw is so positioned that it permits free back-and-forth movement of the firing pin within the limits established by the width of the milled area. Figures 35*C*, *D*, and *E* are free-floating firing pins. All these firing pins are for use with rebounding hammers.

Drill rod is an excellent steel for firing pins. Either water or oil hardening is suitable. The pin should be tempered about the same as a spring. Between 600° and 620°F is the best tempering temperature. In a pinch, I've made firing pins from 1018 or 1020 cold roll steel and case-hardened them. None of them ever came back to haunt me, so I can only assume that this works well. The preference, however, would be drill rod.

If the broken firing pin is still in the shotgun, it is easy to determine the shape and dimensions. Merely remove it and "mike" the remnants. If the pin is completely missing, it's still not too difficult to get

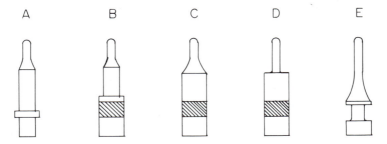

Figure 35. Various firing pin configurations encountered in break-open shotguns. Even if the pin is missing, you can reconstruct its dimensions and shape.

the body diameter, length, and shoulder shape. Clean out the body hole thoroughly with fine steel wool saturated with WD-40 and wipe clean. Using a solvent, wipe the breech face clean of any oil. Put a piece of Scotch tape across the breech face to cover the firing pin hole. Cut a round toothpick in half. Try it in the firing pin retaining hole. If it fits snugly, fine. If not, wrap it with Scotch tape until it does. Now insert the toothpick into the retaining pin hole until it *just* protrudes into the firing pin body hole. This is to ensure that all holes are plugged and dammed, because a cast will be made of the hole. On a slightly concave piece of aluminum foil, with one end shaped into a channel, melt a small amount of paraffin or candle wax over the kitchen stove. Pour the melted wax into the firing pin body hole. When it has solidified, remove the toothpick. With a narrow-blade knife, cut the wax around the hole flush with the surrounding metal. Remove the Scotch tape from the breech face. Using a nail or similar metal rod of slightly less diameter than the firing pin hole, with the end ground perfectly flat, gently tap the wax casting out of the receiver. The tip will most likely be distorted, but this is of no consequence. You now have a fairly accurate reproduction of the body dimensions and the shoulder shape. Using your vernier or dial calipers, measure the distance from the breech face to inside the receiver where the hammer makes contact with the firing pin base. Adding 0.058 inch to the measurement will give the completed overall firing pin length.

Select a piece of drill rod slightly larger than the largest firing pin diameter. Cut off a length about two and a half times as long as the total firing pin length. Using your newly constructed lathe, insert the drill rod in the chuck to a depth of about one firing pin length. With the round nose tool, turn the entire length to a diameter of about 0.015 inch larger than the final desired diameter. Next, use one of the flat sides of the pointed tool to bring the diameter to within 0.005 inch. (The final diameter will be 0.002 inch less than the diameter of the wax cast.) With an 8-inch smooth mill file, bring the drill rod to its final diameter. The firing pin tip will be turned next. Measure the length of the wax cast from the base to the shoulder. Subtract this from the previously determined overall firing pin length. The difference will be the tip length. Add about 0.125 inch to this length to allow for adjustments and filling, and lay off the distance on a firing pin blank. (Do not remove the blank from the chuck until all turning is completed. Chances are it could not be returned to the chuck again and turn true.) Depending on the shape of your firing pin shoulder, you may want to grind another turning tool with a smaller radius than the one you have been using. When the proper tool has been determined, turn the tip in the same manner the body was turned. Give the final shape to the shoulder with the appropriate files. When all filing has been completed, polish the pin with No. 220 and No. 320 wet-dry silicone paper while it is rotating.

Remove the firing pin from the chuck, and try it in the gun. It should slide back and forth smoothly, with a considerable amount of the tip protruding when it is in its maximum forward position. Remove the firing pin and coat it with a layout fluid. Insert the pin into the gun again to its farthest forward position, and with a scribe, scribe a line around its circumference just even with the surrounding metal. With a hacksaw, cut off the surplus drill rod so that the scribed line just shows. Return the pin to the lathe, and with the pointed turning tool flat edge, "face" the base of the pin. Return the pin to the gun, in its farthest forward position. Using the depth-measuring part of your vernier or dial calipers, measure the distance from the tip to the breech face. From this distance, subtract 0.058 inch. Lay out the difference from the tip, and again cut off the excess with a hacksaw, or if there isn't enough to cut with a hacksaw, straight file it almost to the scribed line. Return the firing pin to the lathe, and with an 8-inch smooth mill file, file a hemispherical tip to the scribed line. Return the firing pin to the gun. With the pin in its farthest forward position, the base should be flush with the surrounding metal, and the tip should protrude 0.058 inch.

The next step is to cut out the recess for the retaining pin or screw. Recoat the firing pin with layout fluid and insert it into the gun. With the pin firmly held in its farthest forward position with the tip of the thumb on its base, use a small needle inserted in the retaining pin or screw hole to scribe the outline of the hole on the firing pin. Now with a flat piece of metal held firmly against the breech face over the firing pin hole, press the firing pin forward so that the tip rests against, and is restrained by, the flat piece. Again, with the small needle, scribe the outline of the retaining pin hole on the firing pin body. The extreme distance between the two scribed circles is the position of the recess. Mark these points with a light file mark. The recess is flat all the way across, and usually of a depth almost half that of the body diameter.

(This you'll have to play by ear.) Ensure that the retaining pin or screw, when in place, allows free movement of the firing pin, but don't go any deeper than you have to. This is a weak point of the firing pin.

LOOSE BARRELS

Next to the broken firing pin, this is probably the second biggest problem with break-open shotguns. It happens to expensive, well-made shotguns as well as lower-priced ones (but not as easily). Excessive looseness of the barrel will cause excessive headspace — a situation that is dangerous to the shooter as well as those in his immediate vicinity.

Looseness can occur because of wear in one, a combination, or all of the following parts (figure 36): the hinge pin; the barrel lug where it engages the hinge pin; and the bolt notch; the bolt. Usually, all of them are well worn. Figure 36 represents a typical single-barrel shotgun. This particular one is of a no-name brand and bears only the lettering LONG TOM. It does have a 36-inch barrel and is surprisingly well made. There is little variation in the shape and placement of the various parts of different break-open shotguns. (That doesn't necessarily mean that they're interchangeable, though.) On some shotguns,

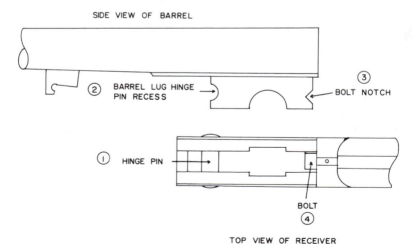

Figure 36. A view of the receiver and barrel-lug assembly of a typical single-barrel break-open shotgun. The critical wear points are the barrel-lug hinge pin recess and bolt notch, and their counterparts in the receiver, the hinge pin, and bolt.

the bolt notch may be rectangular rather than the V shown in figure 36, which depicts the barrel assembly positioned directly over the receiver as it would fit if the two were assembled. In any loose gun, it can safely be assumed that wear would occur on the right-hand and top side of the hinge pin, the entire surface of the lug hinge pin recess, the lower half of the bolt notch, and the bottom of the bolt. Wear on the hinge pin assembly would cause sloppiness in a direction parallel to the axis of the bore. Wear on the bolt or bolt notch would cause sloppiness in an up-down direction, as though you were trying to break the gun open with the bolt engaged.

The classic method of dealing with these ailments in the hinge pin assembly is to bore out the old hinge pin, clamp the barrel in its proper position, and ream out the hinge pin hole and lug recess to a larger size. A new hinge pin is then pressed into place. The bolt notch is built up with weld, and remachined, as is the bolt. It sounds simple when described in a few sentences but it is a delicate, costly process. For a higher-grade Parker, L. C. Smith, Purdy, or Manton, the job would be well worth the cost. For the type of shotguns we're concerned with, such an operation would be ridiculous. There is a more simple, less expensive method of correcting these faults that can be executed with a minimum of equipment. It involves shim stock, trial and error, and a little solder.

Shim stock is accurately sized sheet metal. It is available either in steel or brass. For our use, steel is recommended. It is made in thicknesses from 0.001 inch to about 0.035 inch, in increments of 0.001 inch. Most industrial supply houses carry it in rolls, individual sheets, or an assortment of small sheets in all of the various thicknesses. The last is the most useful to the gunsmith or mechanic for gunsmithing and any general shopwork.

Start with a piece of shim stock 0.005 inch thick. Cut off a piece the width of the barrel lug thickness, and the length about ¼ inch greater than the width of the barrel lug (figure 37A). This shim stock must be converted into a shape that will conform with the barrel lug face and recess (figure 37B). Since shim stock is rather springy, it is difficult to do this precisely with the tools available, so make an attempt with your fingers. All that is necessary at this point is that the shim stock be shaped so that it can be positioned approximately over the face, with some of it in the hinge pin recess. With the barrel held vertically, lay the shim stock on the lug face. Hold the barrel steadily during the

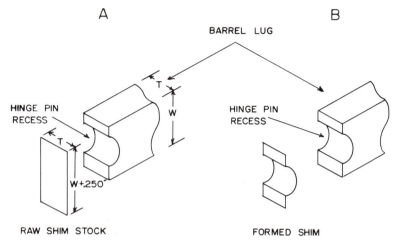

Figure 37. Shaping shim stock to take up looseness on a worn hinge pin and hinge pin recess.

next step, or you'll be looking for the shim stock on the floor. Carefully place the hinge pin over the shim stock and close the gun. Put the fore end in place and open and close the gun a few times. The shim stock will now be perfectly shaped. If you have difficulty in closing the gun, your shim stock is too thick. Try one 0.001 inch less. If it is still sloppy, go for 0.001 inch more. Repeat this procedure until you can just close the gun and then make your final shim 0.001 inch less in thickness. There is no need to solder this shim in place. It will stay there by itself as long as the gun is together. Just remember that it is there when you disassemble the gun, however, or you might wind up making a new one.

The shim on the bolt notch will be soldered. Again starting with 0.005 inch shim stock, cut out a piece larger than the bottom area of the bolt notch. Take a piece of plain wire solder (*not* flux core) and pound about an inch of the end flat and thin. Thoroughly clean the bolt notch and the shim stock with a solvent to remove all grease, oil, and residue. With a cotton swab, paint the bottom of the bolt notch with liquid soldering flux. Be careful that you don't overdo it, or you'll have solder adhering all over. Carefully lay the shim stock in the notch so that it completely covers the bottom. Apply heat to the lug just forward of the notch with a propane torch. You'll need three hands for this job, so find someone to assist you. Have that someone hold down the shim stock with a flat piece of metal, like a screwdriver. While you are applying heat, hold the pounded-thin solder at the bottom of the shim stock and against the lug. As soon as the solder melts, you'll see it seep between the lug and the shim stock. Remove the heat and wait until everything cools. Make sure your assistant has a steady hand, or the soldering job will be ruined.

When the shim stock and lug are cooled, dress the shim stock down so it is flush with the lug on all sides and all excess solder is removed. Reassemble the gun with the hinge pin shim in place, and close it. In all likelihood, the top lever will not return to the fully closed position. This is good. If it does return, replace the notch shim with thicker shim stock. The top lever should return only about half way. When you finally have the right thickness, coat the bolt face with Prussian blue. Reassemble the gun and close it. Give the top lever a light push in the direction of closing. Remove the barrel from the receiver and examine the bolt notch. The Prussian blue from the bolt should have transferred to the notch at the contact point or points. With a 6-inch No. 1 barrette file, file off the high spot or spots where the Prussian blue transfer occurred. Repeat this procedure until the top lever closes smoothly all the way.

You now have a shotgun with a new firing pin and a tightened-up action. This gun can serve as a utility or back-up shotgun for another fifty years — or until a spring breaks. Springs will be covered in chapter 16.

SIGHT MOUNTING

Until 1968, millions of surplus military rifles from numerous countries were imported into the United States and sold to shooters and sportsmen at bargain prices. They were truly bargains. Strong, reliable, accurate shooters, they became the deer rifles of an army of American hunters. Even today, a walk in the woods during deer season will give an indication of just how many are still in regular use — some with minor alterations, some with major custom work, and most with the exact same look as when issued to some foreign soldier fifty years ago. Almost all of these have one minor fault in common: the open rear sight. On a ranking of the three kinds of sights available for rifles (telescope, peep, and open), the open sight rates a poor third. This becomes markedly apparent as you reach middle age and develop a need for reading glasses. With an open sight, it is necessary to fix on three points: the rear sight, the front sight, and the target. To the middle-aged eye, the whole mess becomes a blur. With a peep sight, one looks through the hole in the peep and concentrates on the front sight and target. A much clearer sight picture is realized. A scope, of course, would be even more preferable as a sighting instrument, but most old military rifles need a major bolt handle alteration before they can accommodate a scope. To keep it simple, inexpensive, and practical, we'll go with a receiver peep sight.

As a rule, most receiver peep sights are affixed to the receiver with two 6-48 screws. Most sights are mounted on the right-hand side of the receiver bridge just forward of the bolt handle. (This does not hold true for receivers with a split bridge where the bolt handle winds up in the middle of the receiver, such as the Russian Mosin-Nagnet, or the Manlicher-type receiver. These need a different type of sight.) On flat-sided receivers, such as the Winchester 92 and 94 or the Marlin lever action, the sight is mounted on the left side of the receiver, just forward of the hammer. Though almost all the newer commercial rifles — bolt action and lever action, high-powered and .22 caliber rimfire — are drilled and tapped for just about any kind of sight, their older versions might not be.

The problems with drilling and tapping for any kind of sight are establishing and maintaining proper alignment of the sight relative to the axis of the bore and the horizontal reference plane, and accurately laying out, drilling, and tapping the screw holes. The busy professional gunsmith of today uses a fixture for this purpose. However, these fixtures are expensive and economically impractical for the amateur. The old-fashioned method is longer and more tedious and can result in errors. However, if properly and carefully executed, it will be error-free and the final results will be entirely satisfactory.

Modern receiver sights are accurately machined. Almost always that portion of the sight that will be anchored to the reciever will be a perfect fit with the receiver (unless a significant amount of metal has been removed from that area of the receiver). This accurate fit will provide for half of the first alignment requirements: proper alignment with the axis of the bore. The second requirement of alignment with the horizontal plane will be established by the gunsmith. In figures 38*A* and *B*, note that the bottom of the receiver is flat. The bolt rails

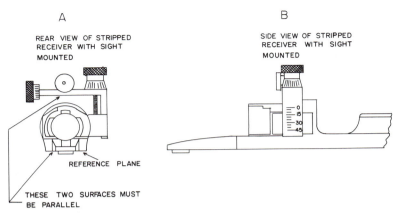

Figure 38. The proper position of a receiver sight relative to its reference planes.

are parallel with the bottom of the receiver. This flat bottom, then, becomes the reference plane.

Strip the barrel-receiver assembly of all attached parts. Take a piece of two-sided adhesive tape (the kind used to hold down carpeting), and place a piece on the receiver bridge over the area where the sight will be attached. Lightly clamp the barrel-receiver assembly in a vise with padded jaws, in a horizontal position. It will now be possible to level the flat bottom reference plane in a horizontal position. An accurate machinists' level will be necessary to accomplish this. With the level flat against the flat receiver bottom as in figure 39, rotate the barrel-action assembly until the bottom flat is perfectly level. Now, holding the level against the receiver bottom lengthwise, level the barrel-receiver assembly in that direction. Return the level to the first position, as shown in figure 39, to ensure that the position didn't change while the second leveling was taking place. Tighten the vise so that the assembly is solidly held and check the leveling again. It may appear that we're overdoing the level checks, but remember, you have only one shot at properly mounting the sight. If this initial setup is not perfect, the job will be botched, and you will have little chance of correcting it.

Strip the receiver sight as shown in figure 39. With the level now lying across the top of the sight frame, carefully bring the contoured

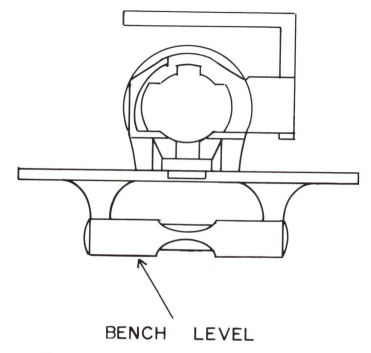

BENCH   LEVEL

Figure 39. Use a level to arrive at the desired reference plane.

portion of the base against the receiver bridge and press it against the
two-sided tape. Rotate the level 90 degrees so it is parallel with the
bore axis, and check the leveling in that direction. Make all necessary
adjustments, constantly checking for levelness in both directions.
When satisfied that the sight is level in all directions, clamp the sight
base to the receiver with an appropriate-size toolmakers' clamp.
Again check with the level to ensure that the base did not shift while
clamping.

It is now possible to locate the first screw hole. Many receiver sights
have one screw hole located through the dovetail part of the base and
one through the thickest part of the base, outside the dovetail. For the
initial hole to be drilled and tapped, use the hole through the thickest
part of the base. This hole will also serve as a guide when tapping.

The sight I have in front of me is an old Lyman Model 57, for the 98 Mauser. The screw holes are 0.144 inch in diameter. This would be the body drill size for a 6-48 screw or a No. 27 drill. Next, make a punch mark on the receiver exactly in the center of the sight base hole. For this a special prick punch will be made. If you don't have any carbon steel drill blanks, get an assortment from an industrial supply house. They are inexpensive and extremely handy for such things as punches, firing pins, and pins.

If the screw hole in your sight is for the 6-48 screw, select a No. 27 drill blank, anneal it, and cut off about 1 inch. Set the length of drill rod in your homemade lathe, and turn a 60-degree point on it, being careful that the point is centered. Harden the piece, polish it, and draw it until the color just turns blue. We now have our special punch.

Insert the punch in the screw hole, and hit it smartly with a hammer — *only once*. Visually check that the punch mark is in the center of the hole, then return the barrel-action to the vise, level it, and check the sight for squareness. If all is square, plumb, and level, the receiver is ready for drilling. If not, go back to square one and make it so. Remember, your sight job rests on this hole.

Remove the sight and tape from the receiver, and deepen the prick punch mark with a center punch. If you have a drill press or access to one, put the receiver in the drill press vise with the flat bottom against one of the jaws, and drill the hole completely through the receiver side with a No. 32 drill. If you're using a hand electric drill, have someone with sharp eyes checking your drill alignment for squareness. When the hole is drilled, put another piece of two-sided tape on the receiver, with a hole cut out around the just-drilled hole. Go back to step one, of leveling, attaching the sight to the tape, and clamping. Only this time, before attaching the sight base to the receiver, insert the 6-48 tap through the body and into the drilled hole so as to align the holes properly. While the tap is just started in the hole, level the sight and clamp it with the toolmakers' clamp. Thread the hole, then insert the receiver sight screw and tighten it.

The second hold will be spotted with a No. 27 drill. Return the barrel-receiver to the drill press or vise, with the sight base held firmly in place with the one screw. With a No. 27 drill, drill the second screw hole just to the point where a mark appears in the center of the screw hole about as deep and as wide as a center punch mark. Shift to a

No. 32 drill, and using the spot just drilled as the center, complete drilling through the receiver side. With the sight base still in place, tap the second hole using the sight base hole as a guide.

In all likelihood the sight base screws will be too long when fully tightened and will protrude into the receiver, obstructing the bolt. It will be necessary to dress these screws until they are flush with the inside of the receiver wall.

SIGHTING-IN

In the interest of economy of ammunition, I like to start the sighting-in process at 25 yards. (I've seen rifles that wouldn't hit a 3-foot-square target at 100 yards.) The target should be a 3- or 4-foot-square, clean, blank sheet of cardboard or wrapping paper.

Inscribe a cross with a black heavy felt tip pen the full length and width of the target paper. The sighting-in should be done from a bench. With sandbags just forward of the trigger guard and just behind the pistol grip, adjust the rifle so that the line of sight is exactly on the center of the target cross. The line of sight should remain fixed on this point without your having to touch the rifle. Being very careful not to disturb the gun as it rests on the sandbags, assume your shooting position and crank out three slow rounds, all aimed at the center of the cross. At 25 yards, any rifle will shoot a tight group.

If the center of your group lies about a couple of inches above the horizontal line, and pretty much on the vertical line, you're in luck, and can move the target out to 100 yards. If it's anywhere else on the target, you must now adjust your sights. As an example, assume that the center of the group is 3 inches to the left of the vertical line and 2 inches below the horizontal line. At 100 yards the error would be magnified four times. The center would be 12 inches left and 8 inches low (and more, because of the greater drop of the bullet).

Adjustments with a scope are quite easy to perform. The adjusting knobs have an arrow pointing in a certain direction, whether movement in that direction will cause the point of impact to move up or down, right or left. Different scopes may have different increments of adjustments. Let's assume your scope has one-minute increments. That means that for every click on the adjusting knob, your point of impact will move 1 inch at 100 yards. In the above case, it would require twelve clicks to the right and eight clicks up to bring the point of impact on target.

The rules for movement of any iron rear sight are as follows:

- If you want the gun to shoot to the right, move the sight to the right.
  - If you want the gun to shoot to the left, move the sight to the left.
  - If you want the gun to shoot higher, raise the sight.
  - If you want the gun to shoot lower, lower the sight.

As a general rule for all iron sights, you will adjust only the rear sight. If the front sight must be adjusted, there is usually something wrong. In all probability, the sight has been damaged or forced from its proper position.

Most receiver peep sights have quarter-minute click adjustments. In the example above it would require forty-eight clicks moving the peep to the right and thirty-two clicks moving it up.

After the sights have been adjusted to bring the point of impact on target at 25 yards, move the target out to 100 yards and repeat the procedure. I like my rifles sighted in at 100 yards; some shooters prefer 200 or 250 yards. This is a matter of personal preference.

10

Action Tune-Up

Most rifles and handguns are far more accurate than the average shooter using them. Though it is obvious that no human being can hold a gun on target with the steadiness and rigidity of a machine rest, certain features, or lack thereof, greatly contribute to the inability to squeeze off a well-aimed shot at the target. Perhaps the most important of these features is trigger pull. To hold a gun, rifle, or handgun steady in an off-hand position with the sights accurately aligned on target is somewhat of a physical feat. The second major physical effort in the drama is squeezing the trigger. Nothing can be so disconcerting and disturb the aim so much as a heavy, long, "gravelly" trigger pull.

TRIGGER THEORY

A proper trigger pull for a single-stage trigger should be a smooth, clean break. There should be no noticeable travel of the trigger, either smooth or rough. When the predetermined release pressure is reached by the trigger finger, the break between trigger and hammer should be instantaneous and clean. Three factors must be met to arrive at this end: proper angle of engagement between the sear and hammer notch; total area contact between the sear and hammer notch; and smooth, polished surfaces making the above contact. Figure 40*A* is a sketch of a hammer and trigger from an old Remington Hepburn falling block single-shot rifle. In this example, the hammer and trigger engage directly. Figure 40*B* is a blowup of the notch-engagement area. Note the arc swung from point *A*, the trigger pivot pin hole center. While the trigger is fully engaged, all pressure from the hammer notch will be directed against the trigger nose in a direction parallel to the dotted line *A–B*. There will be no tendency to cam the nose either up or down. As the trigger is squeezed and the nose is depressed, point *B* will follow the path of the arc until disengagement. While this is taking place, there will be no hammer movement until disengagement.

Figures 41*A* and *B* illustrate in exaggerated form the two incorrect angles. In figure 41*A*, while the trigger is fully engaged, the tendency of the hammer notch is to force the nose in an upward direction and wedge it into the notch. As the trigger is squeezed, point *B* will follow the path of the arc until disengagement. As you can easily see, this

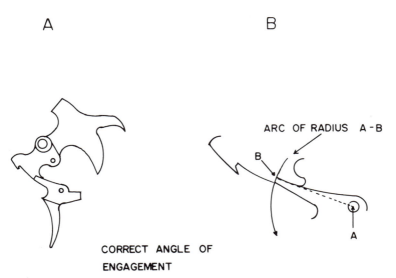

Figure 40. Angle of engagement of the sear-hammer of the direct engagement type. This principle holds true for any type of sear-notch engagement.

A   B

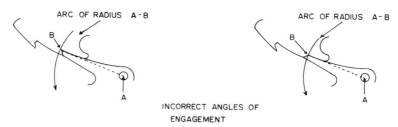

INCORRECT ANGLES OF
ENGAGEMENT

Figure 41. Two incorrect angles of engagement. *A* would cause the hammer to be cammed when the trigger was squeezed; a smooth, light trigger pull could never be achieved. *B* would cause the hammer pressure to cam the trigger sear tip down; the sear would disengage the hammer notch with little or no pressure on the trigger—a most dangerous situation.

will create a camming action against the hammer notch, causing the hammer to be rotated clockwise against hammer spring tension. The trigger pull in this situation can never be lightened regardless of how smooth and perfectly mated the contact areas may be.

The exact opposite is the case in figure 41*B*. The back pressure from the hammer notch would have a component force in a downward direction against the trigger. This would have the same effect as light finger pressure against the trigger. This kind of an angle of engagement can be dangerous, precipitating an accidental discharge of a cocked gun. Should the gun be accidentally struck against some object, inertia acting against the trigger could generate enough force, coupled with the downward camming action, to overcome the friction between the hammer and the trigger. The result, again, would be accidental discharge.

Figure 42*A* is a front edge view of the trigger and hammer side view in figure 42*B*. The projection lines extending from *B* locate the corresponding point on the end view. The shaded area on the end view illustrates improper mating of the trigger and hammer notch. The trigger has been stoned at an angle. The tendency in this situation would be for the trigger to dig into the hammer notch surface.

The above principles apply to all conventional sear and notch applications, whether they are of the direct contact type just illustrated or the type arrangement of the Model 1911 Colt .45 automatic. They apply to rifles of the hammer-type illustrated in figures 40*A* and 42*B* and to handguns. Trigger work for bolt-action rifles will not be covered. For a number of years replacement trigger assemblies have been commercially available. These replacement triggers are available for just about any high-powered rifle. They are truly precision instruments at a reasonable price and need no customizing. Though the pull of any military rifle trigger can be improved, the performance of these replacement triggers is so superior that it would be senseless to mess with the old trigger. Most new production bolt-action rifles are factory-equipped with this type of trigger.

STONING

The object of stoning and sear and hammer notch is to obtain smooth, true surfaces. In the case of revolvers, removing too much metal on either the sear or the hammer notch, or both, could result in throwing off the timing. Exercise care that you don't overdo it. There

A   **B**

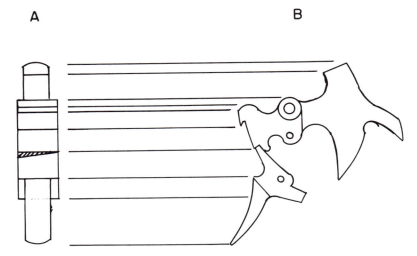

Figure 42. The shaded area in *A* illustrates improper contact between the sear and hammer notch. Full contact is mandatory along the entire width of the sear and notch.

are several jigs or fixtures currently on the market designed to stone sears and notches. They make a first-class trigger job almost routine, and the professional gunsmith doing a lot of trigger work without one is throwing money away. However, they are expensive and it would be difficult to justify the cost for only an occasional job.

In dealing with a quality handgun, such as Colt, Ruger, or Smith & Wesson, it can almost be safely assumed that the angle of engagement is correct and that total area contact between notch and sear exists . . . almost, but not always. The fact that the gun needs a trigger job indicates that something is wrong. The first step is to examine the notch and sear contact. For this purpose, a fixture that will hold the hammer and trigger-sear in the exact same position as they are in the gun will be necessary. This is easily made from two short lengths of drill rod and a flat block of cold roll steel ½ inch thick and 2 inches square. The drill rod must be the same diameter at the pivot of the hammer-trigger-sear. Determine the distance between the hammer pivot hole, and the trigger-sear pivot hole. Sometimes this can be done by partially inserting the hammer pivot and trigger-sear pivot into their respective holes and measuring the extreme distance (on the outside of both) between them. From this distance, subtract half the diameter of each. Often it will be necessary to measure the extreme distance between the pivot holes on the frame using the inside dial or vernier calipers. As above, half the hole diameters are subtracted from the distance.

Spray or paint one side of the cold roll steel block with layout fluid. Select a spot on the block for the hammer pivot hole, and lightly make an indentation with a prick punch. Set your vernier or dial calipers to the distance determined above, and lock them at this setting. Using the prick punch indentation as center and the pointed inside measuring part of your calipers as a compass, swing an arc in an area that will accommodate the trigger-sear. Carefully prick punch anywhere on the arc that will allow room for the trigger-sear. Deepen the prick punch marks with a center punch.

If you have a good selection of carbon steel drill blanks, you can usually come up with a couple that will be perfect for the hammer pivot and trigger-sear pivot holes. Drill the holes in the cold roll block slightly undersized and ream to the size of the pivot pins. (A drill press should be used, because it is necessary to have the pivot pins as square as possible with the block.) Using your homemade lathe and an 8-inch smooth mill file, fit the pivot pins into the holes so that light hammer pressure will be necessary to drive them in. (Be careful not to damage them in the process.)

Place the hammer and trigger-sear in place on the fixture, and with the sear fully engaging the full cock notch, apply finger pressure to the hammer as though to rotate it to the fire position. With a strong magnifying glass, under a strong light, ensure that contact is made for the entire engagement width. If it appears to be so, fine. If not, file the information in your mental data bank for further action. While still maintaining finger pressure on the hammer, slowly disengage the trigger-sear. You should feel no movement of the hammer until disengagement takes place if the angle of engagement is correct. If you feel the hammer moving back against your finger pressure, you have a situation as pictured in figure 41*A*. If you detect a forward movement, the situation in figure 41*B* exists.

If engagement does not occur the full width of the contact area, this is the first fault to correct. Paint the contact face of the trigger-sear with layout fluid to give an indication of exactly where the honing is to be done. Set the trigger-sear in a vise so that only a small amount of the sear is above the vise jaws. Adjust the trigger-sear so that the surface to be honed is parallel with the vise jaws. Using a ½ by ½ by 6-inch medium India stone (aluminum oxide), hit the high side of the trigger-sear. Check constantly to see where you are removing metal. Don't overdo it. In all likelihood, you will need to remove only a few thousandths of an inch. Remove the honed item from the vise and wash it off with alcohol to remove any remaining layout fluid. Put a light coat of Prussian blue on the full cock hammer notch, and return both parts to the fixture. Engage the hammer notch and trigger-sear with sufficient finger pressure on the hammer to effect a transfer of the Prussian blue. Make and break contact between the two several times in order to ensure transfer. Check both the side and edge with a strong magnifying glass. Return the trigger-sear to the vise and touch the high spots, as indicated by the Prussian blue transfer. Check your work constantly with the magnifying glass.

When satisfied that the sear face is parallel with the notch, the next step is to make it a perfect, smooth plane. For this, we'll make our own honing fixture. Referring to figure 43*A*, drill and tap a hole for a 10-32 screw at point *A* on your bench vise. This hole should be so located that a piece of ½-inch round cold roll drilled through the diameter

A

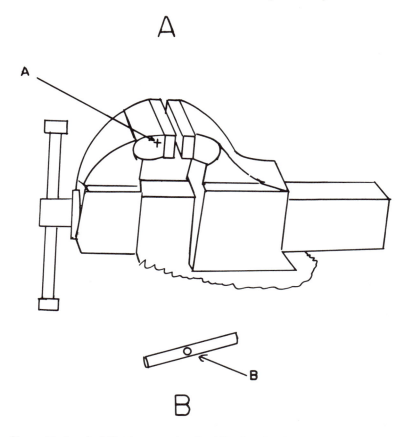

B

Figure 43. A makeshift trigger stoning jig. Affixed to the vise, the rod in *B* is used as a guide and steady rest for the stone.

could be affixed to the side of the jaw with about ¹/₁₆ to ⅛ inch above the level of the jaws (figure 43*B*). Attach the cold roll bar to the side of the vise jaw and, using a small level, level it so it is in a horizontal position and perpendicular to the vertical plane of the jaws. This is the guide that will hold the stone on the proper plane when the trigger-sear will receive its final finish.

Return the trigger-sear to the vise, within 1½ inches of the bar guide. Lay the India stone on the bar, and position the trigger in the vise so the India stone will lie on it at the desired angle. The trigger-sear will then be honed with the stone bearing against it and the guide. When inspection reveals that the honed surface is perfectly flat, mate it against the hammer notch, and effect another Prussian blue transfer. Continue the above procedure, constantly adjusting the angle of contact, until the Prussian blue indicates that there is a reasonable area of contact. The final honing should be done with a fine, hard Arkansas stone.

It has been my experience that the hammer notch seldom needs honing. The only times I have encountered this is when the gun was so old and used that the case hardening had worn through and the notch was deformed. So let's let that area be.

There is one more step to complete on the trigger. It will be noted from figure 40*B* that as the trigger-sear rides out of the notch, as soon as any movement is made, point *B* is the only part that will touch the hammer notch. The super-smooth surface permits a clean break, but point *B* still remains in contact. If this trailing edge were left sharp, as it would be if the previous honing were properly done, it would tend to dig into the hammer notch and cause drag. It is necessary to hone a small radius at this point so it will ride smoothly over the hammer notch.

ACTION WORK

Next to a rough trigger pull, a rough action is the major source of irritation to the shooter. In the case of an avid double-action revolver shooter, such as a bowling pin "nut," it could make the difference between winning and losing. The older prestige handguns were always superbly finished outside and inside. There is clear evidence of much handwork in their final fitting. This is not always the case with their contemporaries. I have on my desk in front of me a relatively new Smith & Wesson Model 34-1 .22 caliber revolver. It was purchased new and has fired approximately 150 to 200 rounds. It is a pea-shooter that I often carry along into the field for plinking. This is a quality handgun commanding a respectable price. In single-action operation, there can be no complaint. The trigger pull is about 3½ pounds, crisp and clean. Although not a double-action shooting aficionado, I do indulge occasionally. Here, the gun falls flat. The trigger finger feels as though it's dragging 60-grit abrasive paper over a screen door. About a week ago the side plate was removed for the first time. Figure 44 reveals the problems. There was no attempt to

Figure 44. One would expect a better grade of workmanship than was revealed when the side plate from my MOD 34-1 was removed. But it provides a perfect example of what to look for in a rough action: *A* and *A'* are the culprits on the exposed side.

eliminate machine marks from the frame or side plate. Burrs and high spots that were present when the frame and side plate came off the milling machine were still there. Note in figure 44 the shiny stripe on the hammer body top (*A*) and a shiny spot (*A'*) on the side plate. Also, note the shiny spot at the top of the hammer just behind the hammer nose. There is a corresponding shiny spot on the frame that can be easily felt with the fingernail and similar shiny spots on the opposite side of the hammer, although not in the same location. The hammer, trigger, hand, rebound slide, and cylinder stop are all nicely finished. The frame was the culprit. This job was easy, because all the original blueing on the frame and side plate was intact, and the color case hardening on the hammer was intact. The only wear is clearly evident in the high areas.

As in the trigger work, the objective in smoothening an action is not to remove a lot of metal but to remove high spots and burrs that interfere with smooth operation. A mirrorlike finish on parts that don't touch accomplishes nothing toward this end. A medium-grit India stone (aluminum oxide) was used for the above job. The small frame made working space quite restricted, so a full-sized stone could not be used. Fortunately, I've accumulated a sizable collection of broken slips, files, and sticks over the years. A broken piece about ¾ inch long of a ⅜-inch-square stone was used on the inside of the frame. The same stone worked nicely on the side plate. After the scratched-up areas on the hammer were smoothened, all the internal working parts were lightly coated with Prussian blue, the gun was fully reassembled, and the action was worked. It felt considerably smoother, but could still stand some work. A second pass at honing was made. The Prussian blue transfer from the parts to the frame revealed only a couple of remaining high spots. The second attempt proved satisfactory, so no further work in this area was done.

The next step was to smoothen the double-action sear-trigger contact points (figure 44, point *B*). It is suggested that the interaction of these two be observed with the side plate removed. With the thumb on the hammer, slowly work the double action. This will give you an idea of precisely where contact is made. These areas should only be polished. For this purpose use 600-grit silicon carbide wet-dry paper.

With older guns, the task of initially identifying existing high spots may be slightly more difficult because of the clutter of old wear, scratches, and machine marks. The gun should be completely stripped and thoroughly cleaned with solvent. When clean, all parts should be given a thorough examination under a strong light with a strong magnifying glass. In the above case it was clearly evident that the problem was a poorly finished frame. However, the fault can just as easily lie with poorly finished internal parts or with both the parts and frame. When you have determined approximately where the problem exists, lightly coat the parts with Prussian blue, reassemble the gun, work the action, and proceed as above.

Although smoothening the action will give a better feel in double-action shooting, it will not appreciably lighten the trigger pull. It will only eliminate that component of pull that was caused by friction and drag. Many double-action shooters, especially competitive shooters, desire a lighter trigger pull. The only way this can be accomplished is with a lighter main spring. Often this is done by clipping a couple of coils off the spring if the mainspring is a coil spring, or grinding some of the bulk off a leaf main spring. I don't recommend this, since it's all trial and error and could easily result in a ruined spring. Light springs are currently available for just about any quality handgun, at a reasonable price. If you feel that you need a lighter pull, go this route. They are specifically engineered, designed, and made for this purpose.

BOLT ACTION WORK

Though not a detriment to accurate shooting, a rough-working bolt action conveys an impression of bottom-of-the-line merchandise, regardless of how well it shoots. The barreled action shown in figure 45 is a Sako L579 in .308 caliber. This is a well-designed, strong action with an excellent barrel. Although this particular piece has never had a round fired through it, there is little reason to suspect that it will not shoot well. Sako has a track record for excellent accuracy; many are capable of minute-of-angle accuracy right off the shelf. The adjustable trigger that came with the action is of the highest quality. For all of its virtues, this Sako has one minor fault that virtually screams at you when working the bolt. The bolt feels as though it is being dragged through gravel. This is not an uncommon fault with many bolt-action rifles.

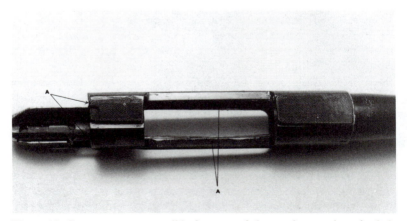

Figure 45. Contact areas responsible for most of the rough operation of a bolt action. The roughness can be worked out, however.

In this case, the bolt has a rather close fit with the receiver. Inspection of the groove in which the locking lugs ride and the bolt rails (*A*) indicate rather pronounced machine marks. It would appear that the broach then in use was approaching its maximum life cycle, and Sako quality control missed this one. The close bolt-receiver fit, compounded by the machine marks, creates a rough operating situation, even though the bolt is highly polished. In addition to the rough broaching job, the bored portion in the receiver bridge still has concentric machine marks perpendicular to the line of travel of the bolt. In an exaggerated sense, this would be comparable to a smooth, round rod sliding back and forth in a closely fitting hole that has been threaded.

Few bolts are as closely fitted to the receiver as the various parts of a quality revolver. Unless you're dealing with a crudely finished military, such as the Arisaki 7.7mm used as a model in chapter 7, the problem is one of rough finish rather than high spots. In the Arisaki's case, it was both.

The job in the locking lug slot and the round portion of the receiver bridge can best be handled with wet-dry silicone 220-grit paper. For the slot, take a piece of wood about 8 inches long, slightly less in width than the slot, and about ⅜ inch thick. Shape one side of the wood to conform to the radius of the slot. Tightly wrap a piece of the 220-grit (one wrap only) around the stick, and sand in a direction parallel to the bore axis. Use a few drops of oil on the paper. This procedure is continued until most of the machine marks are eliminated and then repeated on the other slot. When through with the 220-grit, change over to 400-grit and repeat the procedure.

The bore in the bridge is sanded next. Take a dowel slightly smaller in diameter than the bolt. Wrap a piece of 220-grit around it until it is a snug but movable sliding fit in the receiver. Work it back and forth the length of the receiver in a direction parallel to the bore axis. Do not use a rotating motion. The object is to eliminate the screw marks left by machining, not to establish new ones. Repeat the procedure with 400-grit wet-dry. When done, thoroughly wash out the receiver with a solvent.

The final step is something of a cross between honing and lapping, sometimes called running in. Strip the bolt completely. (If it has a Mauser-type claw extractor, leave the extractor on.) Spread a light coating of 600-grit silicon lapping compound on the bolt. Keep it clear of the locking lug area that engages the receiver when the bolt is closed. Although 600-grit removes very little metal, we don't want to mess with the head space. Operate the bolt in the receiver as it would be used in normal operation until it feels as though it is not hanging up on anything. Remove the bolt and wash both with suitable solvent. The bolt will have a grayish, frosted appearance and should be buffed.

11

A Machined Trigger Guard

Many gun owners have at least one rifle with a stamped metal or aluminum alloy trigger guard they would like to replace with an all-steel, machined guard. If the rifle is a 1903-A3 Springfield or a Model 98 Mauser, they're in luck, because a number of milled guards are still available at reasonable prices on today's gun market. However, with such rifles as the Model 721 or 722 Remington, Model 340 Savage, and a legion of fine, older rimfire .22 caliber bolt-action rifles, the project can become an expensive custom job down at the local gunsmith shop.

The trigger guard is selected as the first make-it-yourself project because often there is need for one; it is relatively easy to make; and it requires application of all the principles of design, layout, drilling, cutting, and filing used in more complex components. The filing involved is a slightly advanced continuance of that described in earlier chapters and is excellent preparation for more advanced projects. The model used for this project will be the Model 75 Winchester .22 LR.

It should be emphasized that the step-by-step procedures described for this particular guard are completely applicable to any make, model, or caliber of rifle having a similar type of guard. Since only the dimensions and some contours may be slightly different, no discussion will be made of dimensions. For your particular gun, they can be easily obtained from the old guard.

There are six steps in the production of the new guard:

1. Design of the guard to exact shape and dimensions.
2. Transferring the design and laying it out on a suitable piece of steel.
3. Removal of the bulk of unwanted metal by drilling and sawing.
4. Rough filing to near finished shape and dimensions.
5. Finish filing to final shape and dimensions.
6. Polishing.

DESIGN

Since we are making a trigger guard to fit on a stock that is already finished, it is necessary that the guard conform as nearly as possible to the contour of the stock. It is usually not practical to trace the old trigger guard and use it as the pattern; often these guards are stamped out to approximately fit a final contour. Because they are made of light metal, they will readily spring to conform to a specific contour when screwed down. The easiest and most practical way to arrive at an exact contour is to trace that portion of the stock, around the trigger guard, on a piece of matte acetate. The reason to use acetate instead of paper or cardboard is that it is hard and tough enough to withstand the treatment it will receive in the layout process.

Lay the stripped-down stock over a sheet of acetate (matte side up) large enough to trace the contour. Leave enough acetate overlapping the bottom of the stock so that the guard loop can be drawn in later (figure 46). With a sharp, soft lead pencil held firmly against the stock and perpendicular to the acetate, trace the contour from a point about ½ inch ahead of the receiver ring screw hole to a point about ½ inch aft of the rear tang screw hole. Draw perpendicular lines through the tracing to mark the exact centers of all screw holes.

The next step is to impose a suitable loop on the contour tracing. This can either be something of your own design or a copy of a loop from another guard that strikes your fancy. I personally like the loop on a 1903 Springfield guard. The position of the loop should be in the

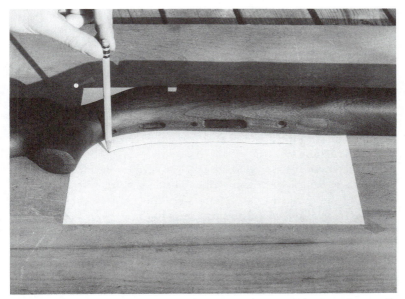

Figure 46. Tracing the stock outline for a new trigger guard. Keep the pencil perpendicular.

same place as that of the old trigger guard, relative to the screw holes. When you have its proper position, trace the loop, superimposing it on the stock contour tracing (figure 46). As a final touch, we'll give some thickness to the base and loop of the guard. About ⅛ to ³⁄₁₆ inch should be sufficient for the base, keeping in mind that the finished guard will be inletted into the stock. Between ¹⁄₃₂ and ¹⁄₁₆ inch should be sufficient for the loop.

Using a straightedge on straight planes and a French curve on the curved contours, smooth up the tracing to its final dimensions and shape. Carefully cut out the finished product with an X-acto knife. This is the exact profile and size of the finished guard.

LAYOUT

Select a piece of mild carbon steel of sufficient size to accommodate the acetate cutout. It should be the same thickness as the widest part of the old trigger guard. Pick one of the long edges as your reference edge. With a straightedge, check that it is straight, and with a machinists' square, check it for squareness with the flats. If it isn't straight and square with the flats, true it up by draw filing. Degrease the bar of steel with a suitable solvent, then paint one flat with a thin coat of layout fluid. When the layout fluid is dry, apply a thin coat of polyurethane varnish over the layout fluid. While the varnish is still wet, carefully set the acetate cutout on the steel flat, with the base straight edge even with the reference edge of the metal. Carefully smooth the acetate cutout to the metal so that complete contact is made, and let the polyurethane varnish dry for several hours.

When the varnish is dry and the acetate cutout is firmly stuck to the steel, trace the outline with a scribe. This outline represents the final profile of the finished guard. Now, we need a second outline of the guard, ⁵⁄₃₂ inch outside of the first outline (figure 47). Set a pair of dividers to ⁵⁄₃₂ inch and, holding one point against the acetate cutout with the other point always perpendicular to the cutout edge, scribe the second outline parallel to the first. This second outline will be used to lay out drill holes.

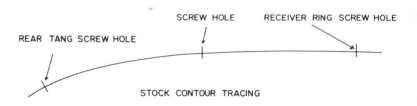

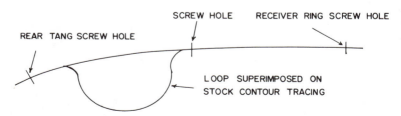

Figure 47. This skelton of the trigger guard will be used to flesh out the final shape and dimensions.

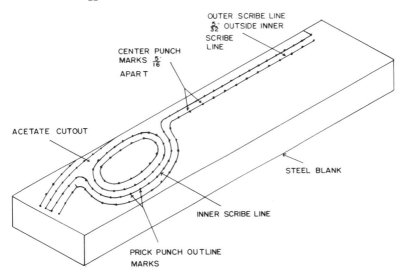

OUTER SCRIBE LINE
$\frac{3}{32}$ OUTSIDE INNER
SCRIBE
LINE

CENTER PUNCH
MARKS $\frac{5}{16}$
APART

ACETATE CUTOUT

STEEL BLANK

INNER SCRIBE LINE

PRICK PUNCH OUTLINE
MARKS

Figure 48. The fleshed-out acetate cutout affixed to a steel blank. The inner punch marks merely mark the outline of the guard. The outer row of punch marks will be used when drilling the blank.

Using a thin prick punch, make light punch marks about every ¼ inch along the periphery of the acetate cutout, on the first scribed outline. The purpose of these marks is to mark permanently the finished outline of the guard. Set a spacing center punch to ⁵/₁₆ inch and center punch the outside outline (figure 48). These punch marks will be used for drilling.

BULK METAL REMOVAL

The amount of bulk metal to be removed is awesome at first glance. The task is greatly simplified by the use of the common twist drill. First, center drill the punch marks on the outside scribed line. After center drilling, drill completely through with a ⅛-inch twist drill. Changing over to a ¼-inch twist drill, redrill the ⅛-inch holes. The reason for this double drilling is to make it easier to drill the final ¼-inch holes. If you have laid out your center punch marks accurately, the final result will be a series of ¼-inch holes, ¹/₁₆ inch apart and ¹/₃₂ inch from the first scribed line outlining the trigger guard. If

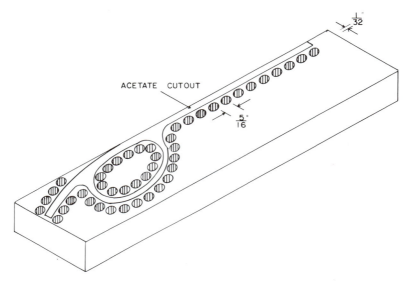

$\frac{1}{32}"$

ACETATE   CUTOUT

$\frac{5}{16}"$

**Figure 49. The steel blank with the acetate cutout attached. On the outside punch
marks, drill ¼-inch holes.**

you have access to a drill press, your work will be greatly lessened. If
not, use a hand electric drill. I've used the hand drill for many years
(figure 49). It's now a relatively simple job to cut through the webs
connecting the series of holes with a hacksaw. The result will look like
figure 50.

ROUGH FILING

While the trigger guard is in the rough, unfiled stage, there is
ample surplus metal to hold it firmly in a vise. However, as it ap-
proaches its finished dimensions, you will encounter more difficulty in
clamping it firmly enough to do the required finishing work. You will
have to secure the guard to a solid base that can be firmly held in a
vise.

The first step will be to finish the bottom of the base completely and
drill the guard screw holes. Using a 12-inch double-cut bastard flat
file, straight file the bulk of the surplus metal from the bottom of the
base until the scribe line is just visible. Finish file by draw filing with a
10-inch second cut mill file until the scribe line just disappears. Paint

the finished surface with layout fluid, and scribe a line the length of the guard, down the center of the base bottom. Locate the exact position of the screw holes, using the old trigger guard as a reference. Drill the holes, using a drill size to accommodate the guard screws. From the opposite side (the base top), countersink the screw holes to a depth where a flat-head screw would be even with the base top when it is completely finished.

Select a piece of hardwood about ½ inch thick, 2 inches wide, and the same length as the unfinished trigger guard. Lay the guard on the wood, with the base bottom close to one of the long edges, and trace the base contour with a pencil. Using either a bandsaw or coping saw, cut out the surplus wood so that the guard base fits in snugly. Secure the guard to the wooden block with wood screws. The trigger guard can now be firmly held in a vise, and all of the exposed metal can be worked on (figure 51).

All rough filing will be straight filing, done perpendicular to the long axis of the trigger guard. For the flat portion of the base and the outside contours of the guard loop, use a 12-inch, double cut bastard flat file. A 10-inch round file, a 12-inch half-round bastard, and a 6-inch half-round bastard will nicely accommodate the curved contours of the loop and the tang. As before, remove the surplus metal so that the scribe lines just show.

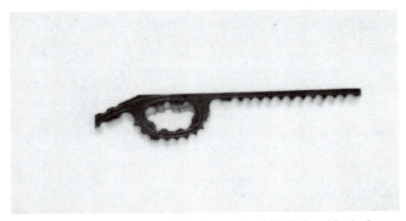

Figure 50. Now cut through the webbing between the drilled holes with a hacksaw.

Figure 51. With the guard bottom filed to finished shape, the guard is mounted on a piece of hardwood. The tang screw was left exposed to indicate the method of mounting. The hardwood base will provide ample surface to clamp in a vise and permit the guard to be worked on without interference.

FINAL SHAPING

Cutting out a slot for the trigger and an opening for a magazine and thinning out the guard loop and tang can best be done after the rough filing. Whether all three functions are necessary in your case depends on your guard. For the example guard, all are necessary.

Remove the guard from the wooden base and check the layout fluid and scribe line on the bottom of the guard base. If they are not reasonably intact, repaint the base with layout fluid and scribe a new line. The magazine opening can be transferred from the old trigger guard. Lay the two guard bases together, back to back, with the screw holes aligned, and scribe the magazine opening on the new guard. For the trigger slot, it is often necessary to ascertain its position and size from the stock. Set the guard in its proper position on the stock, with the guard and stock screw holes aligned. From the inletted side of the stock, scribe the trigger slot on the guard.

Select twist drills $1/16$ inch smaller than the width of the finished slot dimensions. Center punch the center scribe line passing through the slots, using the appropriate drill size to determine the spacing. Center drill, and drill through each slot using the selected twist drills. A rod saw blade, inserted through one of the holes, can be used to cut through the drill hole webs of the magazine slot. For the trigger slot, it will be necessary to use a No. 12 zero cut die sinkers' riffler to file through the webs.

It is a simple operation to insert a file into the slots and straight file the excess metal up to the scribe lines. I find that 4-inch files do the job admirably and are small enough for almost any guard slot work. For the straight filing, use a flat No. 00 cut. For final draw filing, a No. 0 cut is used. The ends of the slots are easily cleaned up with a square No. 0 cut.

On many guards, the tang and the loop are narrower than the front of the base. Determine the final width for your particular guard, subtract this number from the actual width of the rough filed product, and divide by 2. This is the amount that will have to be removed from each side of the tang and loop. In the case of the example guard, the tang and loop will be $7/16$ inch wide. The rough blank is $3/4$ inch wide. Therefore, $5/32$ inch will be removed from each side.

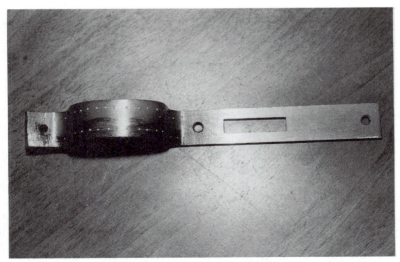

Figure 52. Two rows of punch marks on the loop provide the guide for cutting with a hacksaw.

Degrease the guard, and paint the outside of the loop and the tang with layout fluid. Lay the guard on its side on a flat, smooth surface. Adjust a pair of dividers for the amount to be removed from each side. With one point on the flat surface and the other point perpendicular to the surface, scribe a line around the bottom of the tang. Reverse the position of the guard on the flat surface and scribe a line on the other side (figure 52).

The loop and tang could be filed down to size, but, since we are a lazy lot, we'll do it the easy way and remove the bulk with a hacksaw. Remount the guard on the wooden block, and clamp it in a vise. File a starting notch on top of the guard loop sufficiently outside the scribe line so that the line will show completely when the cut is made. Use a thin saw blade—about 24 teeth per inch. Start your cutting on the guard loop top, and take it around to the tang. Continually check that you are not about to cut through the scribe line. Finish the cut just at the bottom of the front of the guard loop. The front side radius will be filed in. Repeat for the other side. Straight file both sides up to the scribe line.

FINISH FILING

All finish filing will be draw filing. On the front of the guard base and the large outside radius of the loop, use the 10-inch second cut mill file. In the smaller radius at the bottom of the loop, the inside of

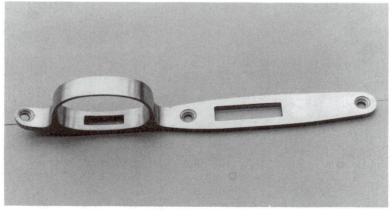

Figure 53. The finished guard is now ready for inletting, polishing, and blueing.

the loop, and the tank, the 6-inch half round bastard works nicely. Draw file all the surfaces until the scribe lines disappear. The last to be draw filed will be the sides of the loop and the edges of the tang and base.

Since the polishing process was covered in a previous chapter, it will not be repeated here. The final product will look like figure 53 — ready for inletting into the stock and for blueing.

12

The Side Lock

The resurgence of black powder shooting during the past couple of decades has verged on the phenomenal. A new industry devoted almost entirely to the production of black powder firearms has developed and prospered during this period. Manufacturers producing buckskin clothing and accessories supposedly duplicating the old frontier style have flourished. Whereas black powder clubs were relatively uncommon some years ago, they are now found in most cities, towns, and villages in abundance. Most rifle, pistol, skeet, and trap ranges formerly devoted entirely to the use of modern arms now boast the addition of a black powder range. Many states have adopted a primitive firearms or muzzle-loading deer season reserved exclusively for this class of firearms. A major manufacturer of modern gun powders has developed a powder for use in muzzle loaders that duplicates the characteristics of traditional black powder but is superior in all other respects. All of this attention showered upon the gun nut with a prospensity for nostalgia indicates one thing: There are a lot of them out there! The reason is simple. It's a fun sport and, when properly practiced, a safe sport.

The development of the hand- or shoulder-held firearm was an evolutionary process. Even the era spanning the height of the percussion muzzle loader and the modern automatic weapon is evolutionary — rapid but nevertheless evolutionary. The first hand or shoulder weapon was the matchlock, which evolved into the wheellock, and then the flintlock. The development of the percussion system marked the transition of propellant ignition from the direct application of fire to the propellant powder, to the ability to ignite it by mechanical percussion. The Reverend Alexander John Forsyth, a Scotsman, is generally credited with making the most significant discoveries involving the percussion system by the application of fulminates to firearm use, around 1807. Many inventions of varying degrees of usefulness for the practical use of fulminates as an igniter immediately followed. Joshua Shaw of Philadelphia is credited with inventing the most practical gadget of all in 1816, the copper percussion cap. This percussion cap is the father of today's modern rifle, pistol, and shotgun primers.

The percussion lock was chosen for the project rather than the flintlock for the following reasons:

• Far more percussion locks than flintlocks are used by the modern black powder shooter.

• It is a simpler and more reliable system.

• The percussion lock can be considered the transition mechanism between the muzzle loader and the modern cartridge rifle or shotgun. With only the most minor alterations, the percussion lock can be used on a muzzle loader, a percussion breach loader, or a rifle or shotgun using modern cartridges. A good example of a cartridge rifle making the transition by using the percussion lock mechanism is the 1873 trapdoor Springfield. Numerous side-by-side double-barrel shotguns and rifles and three-barrel drillings using modern cartridges were made with the hammer percussion lock mechanism. Even today several European makers of fine sporting arms produce a modern side-by-side double shotgun with hammer side locks. A modification, moving the hammer inside the lock plate, is often used on higher-priced European shotguns.

BACK ACTION AND FRONT ACTION LOCKS

Basically, there are two types of side hammer locks, with slight variations: the back action lock and the front action lock, or bar lock. The back action lock has the mainspring (hammer spring) behind the

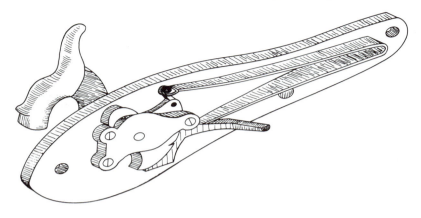

Figure 54. A typical back action lock. Note that the main spring also acts as the sear spring.

tumbler, and the front action, or bar lock, has the mainspring in front of the tumbler. Figure 54 illustrates a typical back action lock; figure 55 illustrates a front action, or bar lock; figure 56 illustrates individual parts nomenclature for both types of locks. The individual parts for both types of locks are basically the same, except that the position of the mainspring swivel, or stirrup, is on opposite sides of the tumbler for the different locks. For the back action lock, the direction of the mainspring force is up. For the front action, or bar lock, the spring force is directed downward. In addition, on the back action lock, the lower leaf of the mainspring is often used as the sear spring; on the front action, or bar lock, a separate sear spring is always required.

The mechanics of operation of both locks is similar and quite simple. Note that the tumblers have two notches. The first notch is the half-cock or safety notch. The loaded and primed gun is carried with the hammer in the half-cocked, or safety position. In this position, the sear is enclosed within the notch. It cannot be disengaged by squeezing the trigger because it is enclosed. The only possible direction the hammer can now be moved is toward full-cock, rotating the tumbler along with it. At this point, the sear engages the second notch. As the tumbler is rotated, it carries the swivel, or stirrup, in a downward direction in the case of the back action lock and in an upward direction on the front action lock. In both cases, the mainspring is compressed. When the trigger is squeezed, an upward force is applied to the right side of the sear, causing it to pivot counterclockwise and disengaging it from the tumble notch. The energy stored in the mainspring is transferred to the tumbler via the stirrup. With the holding action of the sear removed from the second notch, the force of the mainspring is converted into a rotational force by the tumbler and stirrup combination, and the hammer falls. It should be noted that the construction of the half-cock notch must be such that it misses the sear completely when it becomes disengaged from the second notch and the hammer is falling. If it were cut on the same radius as the full-cock notch, the sear would catch on it as the hammer was falling. The placement will be covered in a future chapter.

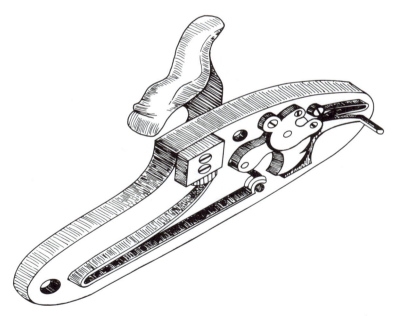

Figure 55. A front action lock. This type always needs a separate sear spring.

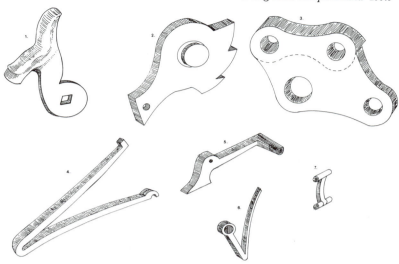

Figure 56. Lock components: 1, Hammer. 2, Tumbler. 3, Bridle. 4, Mainspring. 5, Sear. 6, Sear spring. 7, Stirrup, or swivel.

STRAIGHT-FALL AND REBOUNDING LOCKS

We'll call the locks described above *straight-fall locks*, for lack of a better term. This means that when the hammer falls, it remains at rest on whatever it strikes, still under spring pressure. Straight-fall locks are used on percussion arms. It is important that the hammer continue to press on the percussion cap after the gun has been fired to prevent gas from escaping through the nipple. There is another variation of the lock, called the *rebounding lock*, in which the hammer automatically comes to half-cock after the gun has been fired. This is an important feature when used on firearms employing the modern cartridge. If the straight-fall lock were used, pressure would remain on the firing pin, causing it to remain protruding beyond the face of the breech into the primer. Since modern usage of the side hammer lock is on break-open shotguns and rifles, the protruding firing pin would create a problem when the shooter breaks open the weapon to extract the fired cartridge. With the rebounding lock, the hammer automatically retracts to half-cock, removing pressure from the firing pin it just struck. The firing pin is always under light spring tension in a direction that will cause it to move away from the primer. With hammer pressure removed, it will retract from the breach face.

Figure 57 illustrates a front action rebounding lock. Note that about the only difference from the straight-fall lock is that a portion of the tumbler engages the upper leaf of the mainspring. In the position shown, the lock is in neutral. The sear is engaged at the half-cock position. (Note also that the half-cock notch does not fully enclose the sear as in the case of the straight-fall lock.) The tension of the upper leaf just equals the tension of the lower leaf, leaving the sum total tension on the tumbler at zero. The sear engaging the half-cock notch prevents the hammer from accidentally going forward if struck. However, if the trigger were squeezed and the sear disengaged, the hammer would still not move because it is under zero tension. When the trigger is released, the sear would return to the half-cock notch. The lock is cocked and fired in the same mechanical sequence as the

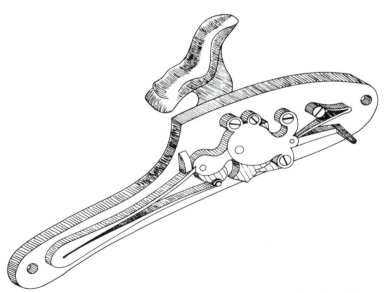

Figure 57. Front action, rebounding lock. Note that about the only difference between this lock and the front action lock in figure 55 is that the upper leaf of the mainspring on the rebounding lock engages a lip on the tumbler arm. This type of side lock is used with rifle-shotguns that use modern ammunition.

straight-fall lock. This time, however, the momentum of the hammer is such that when the lip on the tumbler engages the upper leaf of the mainspring, it will force it down, permitting the hammer to strike the firing pin. When the hammer comes to rest on the firing pin, the tension of the upper leaf rotates the tumbler back to the neutral position, and the sear engages the half-cock notch.

The hammerless side lock is a variation where the tumbler is actually the hammer. This type of lock is used exclusively on modern cartridge rifles and shotguns. There is no half-cock on the hammer. There are only two positions for the hammer: down in the fixed position and fully cocked. The lock is usually of the straight-fall type. The relief of pressure on the firing pin when the hammer is down occurs while the gun is being broken open. A cocking system attached to the underside of the barrel-forearm assembly, and operating through the receiver, engages a lip on the lower front part of the hammer. The instant the gun begins to break, a cocking lever attached to the receiver begins to rotate the hammer to full-cock. This action continues until the sear engages the notch. The spring-loaded firing pins, as with the rebounding lock, retract simultaneously.

For a muzzle-loading percussion firearm, the choice of back action versus front action lock is a matter of choice as to which is more pleasing in appearance. Personally, I think the front action, or bar lock, looks the nicer of the two. I have heard theories attempting to put the selection on a technical plane. One argument is that the back action lock requires the removal of a large amount of wood from the small of the stock, where it is weakest. It can easily be argued that a large amount of wood is removed in the vicinity of the barrel for the front action lock. This, too, is a weak area. But then, opinions are like noses — almost everyone has at least one and they're all different.

The situation is different for a modern shotgun or rifle using a side lock. The front action lock must be attached to the metal receiver. This will necessitate the removal of a large amount of metal from the receiver to accommodate the lock plate and mainspring. Among other things, the cost of production is increased. However, since hammer side locks are used only on double guns of modern manufacture, the front action lock has the advantage of requiring less wood to be removed from the stock, thereby weakening it less. The effects of the back action lock are just the opposite.

13

The Lock Plate

The lock plate is the base or foundation of the lock. Every other part of the lock is attached to and positioned by the lock plate. The lock plate also acts as a bearing for the tumbler on that side of the tumbler that attaches to the hammer. The typical lock plate has between seven and nine holes drilled through it for various purposes. These holes must be accurately positioned relative to each other or the lock will function poorly at best, or not at all. The layout procedure would be relatively simple if the whole gun were designed from scratch on the drawing board. However, since this project entails the construction of a lock for an old, original percussion muzzle loader where the entire lock is missing, purely drawing board procedures are not entirely applicable. A little guesswork will be in order.

Assuming that the lock is the only mechanism missing and that the stock is in reasonably decent condition, there are four reference points available as a starter (figure 58):

• The outline of the lock plate from the inletting of the stock.

• The cylinder to which the nipple is affixed, and the nipple.

• The screw holes through the stock used to secure the lock to the stock.

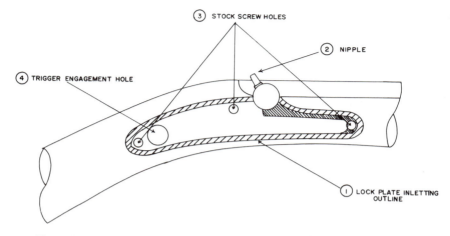

Figure 58. Reference points used in reproducing a lock plate. The stock screw holes and plate outline are fixed and clear-cut. The position of the tumbler arbor hole will require a little guesswork.

• The position of the trigger where it engages the arm of the sear. The outline of the lock plate inletting and the positions of lock screw holes provide exact reference points. The nipple and the point where the trigger engages the arm of the sear provide reference points that, along with some good guessing, will determine the position of the tumbler arbor hole and the sear pivot hole. This will be sufficient to design the tumbler, bridle, sear, and springs. From these the remainder of the holes can be laid out, drilled, and tapped.

PLATE LAYOUT

It will be necessary to have a clean, flat surface around the lock plate inletting. Strip the stock of the barrel, trigger assembly, and trigger guard. Using a sanding block wide enough to cover the inletting completely and overlap the sides, lightly sand the surface around the inletting with 220-grit aluminum oxide paper. Sand only until the edges of the inletting are sharp and clean. Select two wooden dowels about 4 inches long and the same diameter as the screw holes through the stock (usually $^3/_{16}$ or $^1/_4$ inch). Sharpen points on each dowel in a pencil sharpener, making sure the points are centered on the dowels. Using ordinary bright red lipstick, coat the sanded area around the lock inletting with an even, moderately heavy coat. Select a hard, flat surface and lay a section of yesterday's newspaper over it. The newspaper section should be thick enough to provide a light cushion. Lay a piece of plastic drafting vellum, about 4 by 8 inches, on the newspaper. Very carefully, so as not to smear it, press the lipstick-coated stock inletting onto the plastic vellum. While the stock is still under pressure on the drafting vellum, press the pointed ends of the dowels through the stock screw holes with sufficient force to penetrate the drafting vellum slightly. Carefully, so as not to smear the print, remove the stock from the drafting vellum. You should now have a perfect outline of the lock plate with the stock screw holes accurately located. If your gun is like mine, the recess for the cylinder will not appear on the transfer, since the wood on the stock does not extend that far. Simply draw, free hand, a continuation of the plate without the recess. The recess will be cut in later, playing it by ear. (The lipstick should be removed immediately from the stock with a suitable solvent.) Using either scissors or an X-acto knife, carefully cut out the lock plate pattern. The pattern is now affixed to a suitable piece of steel in the same manner as described for the trigger guard in chapter 11.

A word about the steel suitable for a lock plate. If the lock plate were merely a base used to hold various parts in a fixed position, un-heat-treated mild steel would be sufficient. However, it not only fulfills the above function, it also acts as a bearing for the tumbler arbor, which has a strong directional pressure against the relatively thin bearing surface caused by the action of the mainspring. (Additional pressures are transmitted to the lock plate screw holes via the bridle, sear and sear spring, and mainspring stud. It stands to reason that a soft, un-heat-treated lock plate would soon be worn or deformed through normal usage. As in all other parts of the lock (except the hammer and screws), heat treating is mandatory.

Depending on the facilities available, either case hardening or regular hardening and tempering are suitable. For a part as large as a lock plate, a larger volume of heat would be required for case-hardening than regular hardening and tempering. Therefore, the latter is recommended. Either water-hardening or oil-hardening steels are suitable. Since oil-hardening steel has less distortion, and something as thin as a lock plate would be prone to distort, oil-hardening steel is preferred. For the project lock plate, an oil-hardening, flat ground stock $5/32$ by

1 by 5½ inches long was used. The size will vary with different lock plates. Determine thickness by measuring the depth of the inletting as it pertains to the plate, and then adding about 0.025 to 0.03 inch. This additional thickness will permit rounding off the outside of the plate to give it a dome effect when it is finished.

As with the trigger guard in chapter 11, the outline is transferred to the steel, and the screw hole points for the stock screws are center punched on the steel. Proceed to drill, cut, and file the plate outline as previously described. When the finished outline has almost been reached and is still visible, drill and tap the stock screw holes. Usually, the original screws are not available. Even if they are, it is preferable to use new screws. As stated earlier, most screw diameters range from $3/16$ inch to ¼ inch. Use the smallest size that will fill the screw holes in the stock. This would be a No. 10, No. 12, or ¼-inch screw. Since the lock plate is relatively thin, the finest thread is desirable in order to get the most threads in the plate. Thus, the tap size would be 10-32, 12-28, or ¼-28.

FITTING AND SHAPING

The plate is now ready for the final fitting to the stock. This procedure is just the opposite of fitting a stock to a gun. In stock making, a marking agent is applied to the metal and transferred to the wood by wood-to-metal contact, and wood is removed. In fitting the lock plate, the marking agent is applied to the wood and transferred to the metal by contact, and metal is filed away from the plate. This is necessary to retain the original dimensions and shape of the stock. With the stock completely stripped, cover the area around the plate inletting with lipstick, both on the outside of the stock and in the inletting, as was done when transferring the plate outline. Insert the stock screws through the stock and attach the lock plate carefully, so that it may be drawn up against the stock, but not so tight that it will deform or crush the wood. Carefully unscrew the screws and remove the lock plate so as not to smear the lipstick. Depending on how closely the plate was brought to its true shape and dimensions, a lipstick transfer of comparable coverage will appear on the inside of the plate. Insert the plate in the vise with a backing of ¼-inch plywood against the inside of the plate, so arranged that it will not touch and consequently smear the lipstick. With a 10-inch second cut file, draw file the areas on the edge that are covered with the lipstick. Don't go too deep, and be sure that only the areas covered are filed. This is because most lock plate edges are not perfectly square with the surface. They are beveled in toward the stock so that they provide a close wood-to-metal fit but are still easy to remove. Eyeballing the inletting will give a good idea of just how much it is beveled. When all the lipstick-coated metal has been removed, repeat the above procedure and file again. Repeat the procedure as many times as necessary to get a perfect fit. This will occur when the plate is fully seated and the entire edge is coated with lipstick. This is not something that will happen in a matter of a few minutes—even for a master gunsmith. So be patient.

If your lock is a front action or bar lock, as is mine, there is one more step in fitting and shaping the lock plate. This is to cut out that area of the lock plate that fits around the cylinder. Attach the plate to the stock securely with the screws. Locate the barrel and tang over the inletted stock as though you were going to seat it into the stock. Obviously, full seating will not be possible because the unfinished lock plate will not permit the cylinder and barrel and tang assembly to be fully seated. However, the position of the cylinder will provide a rough indication as to where the cylinder recess should be on the lock plate. With the barrel assembly as close as possible to being seated, use a straightedge to scribe a vertical line on the lock plate as close as possible to the center of the cylinder. Now measure the diameter of the cylinder, and scribe a semicircle on the plate of a radius the same as the cylinder, using the scribed vertical line and the top of the lock plate as the center. Return the lock plate to the vise, and using a bastard cut round file of appropriate diameter, straight file the plate to within about $1/32$ inch of the scribed semicircle. Don't go any farther on this first attempt, because the accuracy of the layout is rough, at best. Return the plate to the stock, and seat the barrel and tang assembly as before. This time it should go much farther toward fully seating. An eyeball assessment of the cylinder position on the just-filed recess will give a good indication of where more metal will require removal on the lock plate. Return the plate to the vise and resume filing in the areas obviously in need. Repeat this procedure as necessary until the barrel and tang assembly is *almost* fully seated, being careful not to remove too much metal from the plate. At this point, coat the cylinder with lipstick, and seat the barrel and tang assembly firmly enough to transfer the lipstick to the lock plate. Now, using a second cut round file, file those areas on the plate showing the transferred lipstick. Don't file away too much metal. This is your final fitting, and only the high spots should be hit, lightly. Continue this procedure until you have a good metal-to-metal fit and the barrel and tang assembly is fully seated.

One more step is necessary before going on to make the other lock parts. This is to locate the hole in the lock plate for the tumbler arbor. Two points of reference are available for this purpose: the nipple on the cylinder, and the arbor hole, assuming that it is centered on the narrow portion of the plate. Although these two points of reference are rough at best and most likely will not locate the arbor hole at the exact point of the missing original lock, they can approximate the original position closely enough to build a functional lock. Most arbor holes are vertically centered in the middle of the plate. Sometimes on a narrow lock plate the hole will be slightly higher for a front action lock and slightly lower for a back action lock. This is to provide clearance between the main branch of the mainspring and the stock. However, you can't go too far wrong by locating it in the center. In addition, it has been my observation that on most locks, a line connecting the tip of the nipple and the center hole of the tumbler would make approximately a 45-degree angle with the center line of the barrel bore.

Attach the barrel and tang and lock plate to the stock, using all of the appropriate hardware to ensure that everything is securely in place. Lay the gun on a flat, horizontal surface with the lock plate up. Set a length of 2-by-4, with the wide side vertical, against the top of the side of the barrel (figure 59). This will be your straightedge for laying out the reference line. Your barrel may be tapered. If this is the case, adjust the 2-by-4 so it is parallel with the axis of the bore. Once again, this will be guesswork, but a fairly accurate reference is required because the position of the reference line scribed on the lock plate will be greatly affected if the 2-by-4 is not accurately positioned. Using a 45-90-degree mechanical drawing triangle, set one edge against the 2-by-4 and slide it along until the opposite 45-degree edge is just over the tip of the nipple. Now carefully scribe a line across the surface of the lock plate.

With the 45-degree line scribed, remove the lock plate from the stock. Using your vernier calipers, determine where the scribed line passes through the vertical center of the lock plate by measuring from both the top and the bottom of the plate to a point on the line. This is

Figure 59. Determining the position of the tumbler arbor hole relative to the nipple.

all trial and error. When a point on the line is found that is equidistant from both top and bottom, mark it and center punch it. This is the center of the tumbler arbor hole. (The reason you must locate the vertical center by trial and error method is that the lock plate top and bottom shapes most likely are not the same. What may be the vertical center at one point would not be at any other point.) The hole is now ready to be drilled and reamed to finished size. However, this isn't done until the tumbler has been designed and the arbor size determined. At this point, about all that can be done with the lock plate is done. The screw holes for the bridle and sear pivot will be located with the completed parts in place. The plate will be hardened and tempered after all other work on it has been completed.

14

Tumbler, Bridle, and Sear

THE TUMBLER

The hammer is the star performer of the lock assembly. It delivers the blow to the percussion cap, causing it to detonate. The tumbler, however, is the co-star. It provides a place of attachment for the hammer, converts the linear power stroke of the mainspring into a usable rotary motion, and transmits this rotary power to the hammer. The positions of the notches on the tumbler provide the means of positively controlling the cocking and fall of the hammer. The tumbler must be hefty and large enough to withstand the forces exerted against it and to accommodate the other parts acting upon it. Yet it must be small enough to work within the dimensions of the lock plate. The hammer decides the position of the tumbler on the lock plate. The tumbler, however, determines the size and the position of all the other components of the lock.

The basic design of the tumbler is the same for all the different kinds of locks: the back action and front action or bar, and the straight-fall and rebounding lock. Only minor variations make the difference. It would be a simple matter to convert a tumbler from a rebounding lock to that of a straight-fall lock by merely grinding off the lip that engages the end of the mainspring leaf. The only basic difference between the tumbler of a front action or bar lock and back action lock is that the swivel arm for the former is in front of the tumbler arbor and for the latter is behind the tumbler arbor. Yet the design of this apparently simple device is critical to the proper functioning of the whole lock assembly.

As can be seen from the various lock illustrations in chapter 12, the extremities of the tumbler-bridle-sear assembly come rather close to the bottom and top edges of the lock plate. Also, the main branch of the main spring and the stirrup closely approach the lock plate edge. The lock plate controls the maximum size of the tumbler. The tumble arbor determines the minimum size of the tumbler. Since the arbor is subject to considerable pressure from the mainspring, it must be large enough in diameter to provide sufficient bearing surface in conjunction with the arbor hole in the lock plate to permit smooth operation and reasonable wear. The tumbler starts out as a round disk with the arbor on one side and the pivot on the other side (figure 60). In figure 60, note that a dotted circle is inscribed within the blank and given the dimension D. This is the radius on which the half-cock and full-cock notches will be plotted. The diameter the blank will be turned to is D plus ¼ inch. The larger diameter is necessary to fashion a longer

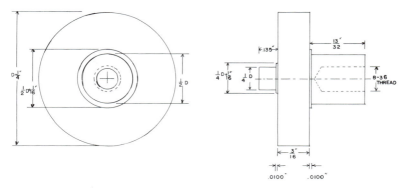

Figure 60. The tumbler blank. This will have to be turned out on a real metal turning lathe.

swivel arm than a diameter of D would permit. The diameter D should be about ¼ inch less than the lock plate width in the area of the arbor hole. This will permit ⅛-inch clearance to the edges of the lock plate, which should be sufficient to seat the lock in the stock fully. The arbor diameter is usually half the diameter of the body, and the pivot diameter is half the diameter of the arbor.

The blank shown in figure 60 is the basis of the tumbler. On its circumference, as modified, the half-cock and full-cock notches are cut, and the swivel arm is fashioned from the remainder of the body. Note that the drawing shows that a shoulder has been left on both the arbor and the pivot. This shoulder is ⅟₁₆ inch larger in diameter than both the arbor and pivot, and 0.010 inch thick. The purpose of these shoulders is to provide a bearing surface against the flat of the lock plate and the flat of the bridle, relieving full contact with the body on both. This provides for smoother lock operation. The arbor has been drilled and tapped for an 8-36 screw.

THE SEAR

The sear is the component that links the tumbler to the trigger. Its purpose is twofold: to restrain the hammer and tumbler in either the half-cock or the full-cock position; and to permit instantaneous, on-demand release of the hammer and tumbler. The placement of the sear and the screw hole on which the sear pivots is critical to the smooth functioning of the lock; the manner in which it engages the full-cock notch on the tumbler determines the quality of the trigger pull. The sear and tumbler designs depend on one another, and while the tumbler is being designed, the nose of the sear will simultaneously take shape.

THE BRIDLE

If any part of the lock could be omitted, it would be the bridle. I have seen cheap locks without a bridle, and they did function — in a rather rough manner. The useful life of such a lock is limited. With the pivot points of the tumbler and sear supported only by the lock plate against strong spring pressures, exaggerated uneven wear and a tendency to distort the tumbler arbor and sear pivot screw would occur. Compare it to driving a car on icy winter roads with worn tires. It can be done, but chains would be more sensible. The bridle provides the necessary support to parts under tension on the side opposite from the lock plate. This is necessary to keep the parts always in perfect alignment by providing a rigid, second bearing surface.

TUMBLER DESIGN AND CONSTRUCTION

The theory of trigger and hammer engagement was covered in chapter 10. This same theory applies to a side lock–sear-tumbler engagement and all aspects of their design will be based on it. A flip of the coin determined that the tumbler for a front action or bar lock would be shown. (Remember, the design principles are the same for a front action and back action lock; the main difference is the position of the swivel arm.) The tumbler blank shown in figure 60 is the basis of the project tumbler. The steel for the tumbler could be either oil-hardening drill rod, or C1020. C1020 case-hardened would work quite well, and the part is small enough to be easily adaptable to home case hardening. The tumbler blank and the bridle blank are the only two parts described in this book that will require a machine tool to produce. It is suggested that you contact your local high school or vocational–technical school machine shop instructor for assistance. If this attempt fails, it will cost only a couple of bucks for the local job shop to make them.

LAYOUT

A little drawing board work and some high school geometry are in order at this point. The half-cock (or safety notch) and the full-cock notches cannot be on the same radius, because there is a high probability that the sear will catch on the half-cock notch as the hammer falls. When the trigger is squeezed and the point is reached that the sear disengages the full-cock notch, further steady squeezing, or lack thereof, will not be fast enough to overcome the speed of the rotating tumbler. Most often, there is a relaxation of trigger pressure at this point. Only an intentional jerk of the trigger will provide the necessary timely displacement to clear the half-cock notch. A radius on a new center for this notch must then be established.

The position of the notches on the tumbler relative to each other and relative to the point where the sear will engage them as they are rotated into position is determined by three factors: the hammer must have a sufficiently long swing as it falls to ensure percussion cap detonation; the half-cock notch must engage and the hammer must have sufficient clearance of the cap or nipple; and the parts on the lock plate must be arranged economically. It's my observation that if a line were drawn from the center of the tumbler to the point on its circumference where the sear will engage a notch, this line would make approximately a 30-degree angle with a vertical line drawn from the center of the tumbler to its circumference (figure 61*A*). The half-cock notch is usually about 30 degrees ahead of the full-cock notch. On figure 61*A*, the sear is engaging the half-cock notch; on figure 61*B*, the sear is engaging the full-cock notch. Geometrically, this 30-degree relationship works out nicely. Since the pivot point of the sear is instrumental in the overall tumbler design, the sear design will be covered, too.

Lay out a circle, as in figure 61*A*, of a diameter of *D* plus ¼ inch. Within this circle, inscribe another one of a diameter of *D*. Circle *D* is the one on which the half-cock and full-cock notches will be plotted. The first notch designed will be the half-cock notch. Note that its position in figure 61*A* is 30 degrees behind a vertical line extending from the center of the circle to the circumference. On the 30-degree line, plot point *A* at a distance of 0.075 inch in from circle *D*. This is about two and a half times the notch depth of the full cock notch (0.030, or about ⅓₂ inch). This depth, on the finished tumbler, will provide the clearance necessary for the sear not to catch on the half-cock notch as the hammer falls and the metal necessary to lock the sear in the recess.

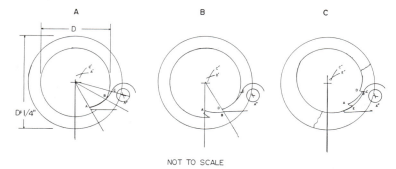

NOT TO SCALE

Figure 61. **Laying out the notches on the tumbler. Note that the radius of the sear conforms to the tumbler radius leading to both the half-cock and the full-cock notches, and to the radius beyond the half-cock notch, even though the angle of the sear is different in all three positions.**

With the compass set to the radius of circle D, using point A as the center, swing an arc outside and to the right of the circle D plus ¼ inch. This is arc A''. At an angle of 15 degrees to the horizontal center line, draw a line from the circle center through arc A''. The intersection is the location of the sear pivot screw center. Set the compass to a radius of ⅛ inch. Using the sear pivot screw center as the center, swing an arc clockwise from the 15-degree line. Where the arc touches the line is point C. Reset the compass to the radius of circle D. Using point A as a center, swing arc A'. Now, using point C as a center, swing arc C'. With the intersection of arc A' and C' as center, swing an arc from point A to point C. We have just established the exact shape, dimensions, and pivot screw center of the sear nose and the tumbler configuration leading to the half-cock notch. Arc $A-B$ cuts the circumference of circle D approximately 32 degrees from point A. Certainly within the ballpark — and acceptable.

Figure 61B illustrates the tumbler rotated 32 degrees clockwise. Locate point D, 0.030 inch (about ½₂ inch) inward from circle D. Using point D as a center, with the compass set to a radius of circle D, swing arc D'. Using point C as a center, swing arc C'. With the intersection of D' and C', swing an arc connecting point D and C. The result is the full-cock notch.

The final step in the notch drama is to lay out the front edge of the tumbler, which provides the clearance after the hammer falls. Figure 61C illustrates the tumbler rotated to the final hammer fall position. This is a position 15 degrees beyond the point of the half-cock position. Locate point E 0.030 inch in from circle D. With the compass set to circle D radius, using point E as center, swing arc E'. Using point C as center, swing arc C'. With the intersection of C' and E' as center, swing an arc from point E until it merges with circle D.

We have just designed the sear nose and located the pivot screw center and that portion of the tumbler involving the notches. Note that the contours of the sear nose and the tumbler are such that they will always make full contact regardless of the angular position of the tumbler. This is necessary to ensure smooth operation and even wear.

Once the above exercises have been performed and understood, the actual layout of the tumbler should be executed using the body diameter appropriate for your lock. Instead of doing the drawing on paper, use drafting vellum or acetate. Execute the layouts of template B and C as above. In addition to the notch layouts, draw a precise circle for the tumbler pivot shoulder. Using an X-acto knife, very carefully cut out the patterns. With a hole punch of the same diameter as the tumbler pivot shoulder, punch out the pivot hole in the vellum or acetate template. Spray or paint the templates with either layout fluid or bright red nail polish. When dry, start with template *B*. Cover the tumbler blank with a thin coat of quick-drying glue, and place template *B* on the tumbler blank, centered on the pivot hole shoulder. When the glue is dry, put the blank in a vise, and using an 8-inch Swiss pattern No. 00 cut pillar file, straight file the edge of the blank *almost* to the acetate or vellum template for both notches. When this point is reached, shift to a 6-inch Swiss pattern narrow No. 2 cut pillar file, and draw file right up to the template outline. Clean up the full-cock notch with a 4-inch No. 2 cut square needle file. The half-cock recess can be cut with a 5-inch No. 00 joint needle file. The same procedure is repeated with template *C*. Now, however, be sure that template *C* is in perfect alignment with template *B*. When filing away metal to conform to template *C*, do not file beyond the broken lines of figure 61*C*. The tumbler body beyond this point will be used to fashion the swivel (stirrup) arm, and in order to obtain the maximum length for the arm, the full tumbler blank radius will be used.

The next step is to fashion a swivel or stirrup arm from the remaining tumbler body and to establish the limits of the tumbler travel. It will be noted from figure 61*C* that the position of the sear is 15 degrees beyond the half-cock notch. At this point, the tumbler has rotated 45 degrees from the full-cock position. This is the point at which the hammer strikes the nipple or percussion cap. To ensure that there is sufficient swing to permit the hammer to strike and that the hammer is under spring pressure after it lands on the nipple, the tumbler and bridle are designed to permit an additional 15 degrees rotation. In other words, if the lock were in place on the gun and the hammer were allowed to fall, the tumbler would rotate to the position in figure 61*C*. If, on the other hand, the lock were removed from the gun and the hammer were allowed to fall, the tumbler would rotate beyond the position in figure 61*C*. The limits of the tumbler travel are determined by the position where a cutout on the tumbler body engages one of the posts on the bridle that anchor it to the lock plate.

On a new sheet of paper, lay out figure 61*C*, but without the arcs, points, and so on. Since we will be swinging new arcs and establishing new points, it's better to start with a clean, uncluttered picture. This is

A B

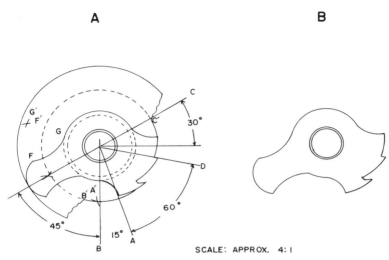

Figure 62. Layout for final tumbler shape. Don't let the apparent clutter throw you.

figure 62. Draw line *A* from the center of the tumbler through the circumference at an angle of 15 degrees to a similar vertical line (line *B*) passing through the center. Where line *A* intersects the circumference establishes the farthest possible point of travel of the tumbler relative to the sear. There will be 60 degrees between the full-cock position and the point established by line *A*. It is obvious now that in order for the tumbler to be brought to full-cock and fall, it must have at least a 60-degree rotation unencumbered by the bridle posts or supports.

The maximum fall limit will be established first. At an angle of 30 degrees to the horizontal, draw line C from the tumbler center to its circumference. Setting your compass to a radius of half the distance between the tumbler circumference and the shoulder turned on the arbor along line *C* (point *C'*), swing an arc that connects the outer circumference and a circle representing the shoulder. When the metal is appropriately removed from the tumbler body, this semicircular cutout will play the tumbler's part in the maximum swing. The bridle post will play the other half. It will be located 15 degrees counterclockwise on the same radius as the tumbler cutout was located and be of slightly smaller diameter than the cutout.

To provide sufficient rigidity to the sear-tumbler-bridle assembly, one more post or support for the bridle is necessary. Its location must be such that it does not interfere with the necessary tumbler movement, yet provide maximum support to the bridle. The optimum for a three-position hold-down would be 120 degrees apart and on the same radius. For a side lock, this is not possible, so a compromise must be made. The compromise will be based primarily on the area and extent of the swing required by the swivel arm, and then on the best location from a strength point of view.

Draw a line *E* from the center of the tumbler through the circumference at an angle of 60 degrees to the vertical line *B*. This will be the axis of the swivel arm. With the compass set to a radius of ⅛ inch, locate *E'* that distance from the circumference (circle *D* plus ¼ inch). Using *E'* as the center, swing a semicircle. Set the compass to a radius somewhat less than the distance between circle *D* plus ¼ inch and the arbor shoulder. From point *F*, locate point *G* on the shoulder, and swing arc *F'*. From point *G*, swing arc *G'*. Using their intersection as center, connect points *F* and *G*. The remainder of the swivel arm contour can be drawn in by hand.

When redrawn to actual size, the template is treated as the previous two. Very carefully align and glue it to the tumbler. Much of the excess metal can be removed by drilling a series of holes approaching but not touching the finished outline in a manner similar to that in making the trigger guard in chapter 11. Straight file to almost finished dimensions. Finish by draw filing.

The square on the arbor and the swivel slot and pivot hole will be covered in a later chapter.

15

Bridle and Sear

In chapter 13 we held in abeyance the drilling and reaming of the arbor hole and drilling and tapping of the bridle screw holes in the lock plate. With the near completion of the tumbler and various layouts of chapter 14, we now have sufficient progress to proceed toward the lock plate completion and bridle design and construction. About half of the sear was already designed in chapter 14.

The bridle blank is one of the project parts for which you need a lathe. Figure 63 illustrates a representative blank. Assuming the ³⁄₈ inch was chosen as the arbor diameter and ³⁄₁₆ inch for the pivot diameter, the following rationale was used to arrive at the dimensions indicated in figure 63. Various portions of the tumbler were taken down to the arbor shoulder diameter, ⁷⁄₁₆ inch. The bridle blank is bored to a diameter of ½ inch to accommodate those portions of the tumbler and to provide a clearance of ¹⁄₃₂ inch on the sides. The depth takes into account the tumbler thickness and the two shoulders, plus 0.005 inch clearance to permit smooth tumbler rotation. The outside diameter is necessarily large to provide sufficient metal to locate the sear pivot screw. The steel can be a low carbon such as 1018 or 1020. The part lends itself nicely to home case hardening.

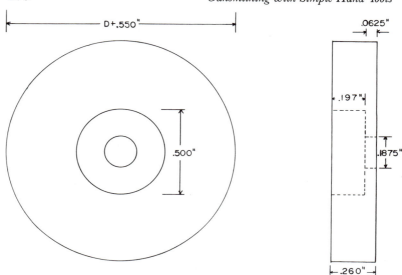

Figure 63. Bridle blank. A lathe will be necessary to produce this blank, as it was with the tumbler blank.

BRIDLE LAYOUT

Now it is necessary to fall back on some data from chapter 14. Referring to figure 64, lay out the sear pivot screw hole using the intersection of the vertical and horizontal cross lines as the reference point. Now strike an arc of a radius of diameter D from the previous chapter. The first hole to be located is the one that anchors the bridle post that limits the maximum hammer fall. Draw line A from the center at an angle of 45 degrees to the horizontal line. The intersection of line A and radius D is the center of that screw hole. The position of this hole is such that it provides an additional 15 degrees free swing to the tumbler before reaching the bridle post when the hammer is resting on the nipple.

The position of the second bridle post screw hole is not as critical from a tumbler control point of view. All that is necessary is that it provide sufficient swing clearance to the tumbler arm, clockwise, so the sear can engage the full-cock notch. It must still be sufficiently displaced from the other post to ensure a sufficient rigidity to the assembly. The screw hole for the sear pivot provides no hold-down support to the bridle. Line *B* drawn at an angle of 60 degrees to the horizontal and arc *D* locate the center of this hole. Sixty degrees was nonscientifically chosen because it will provide a few degrees clearance when the tumbler is in the full-cock position and about the maximum possible displacement from the other post.

We now have enough data and layouts to proceed with the completion of the lock plate. Paint the outside of the plate with layout fluid. Carefully scribe a vertical and a horizontal line, using the center punch mark locating the arbor hole as the center. Using the layout of figure 64, glue it to the lock plate face down (with the sear pivot screw hole behind the arbor hole punch mark), positioning it on the horizontal and vertical scribe lines and the center punched mark. When the glue has dried, prick punch and then center punch the bridle screw hole locations. Remember, the accuracy with which the above is performed will determine how smoothly the lock will function.

The tumbler arbor hole is now drilled and reamed. Use a drill ¹⁄₆₄ inch smaller than the finished, reamed hole. When reamed, de-

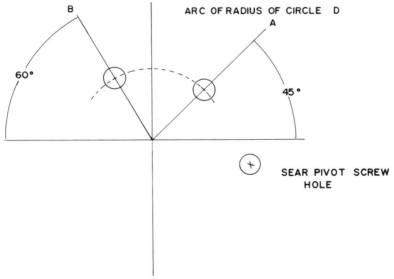

Figure 64. Layout for locating bridle screw holes. This layout will be transferred to the lock plate.

burr the hole on both sides of the plate. Now try the tumbler in the plate to ensure that it rotates smoothly. If it doesn't, check the plate again to ensure that it was properly de-burred. If this is not the problem, put the tumbler in the vise, using soft jaws, and with a strip of 220-grit silicon carbide wet-dry paper about the same width as the arbor length, polish the arbor, using "shoeshine" strokes. Continue this procedure until the tumbler rotates smoothly in the lock plate.

Before the bridle screw holes are drilled and tapped, a few more steps are necessary. The tumbler must be in place on the plate, and the bridle blank must be firmly affixed to the plate. Now it is quite obvious that the raw bridle blank cannot be seated over the tumbler. Some preliminary metal removal from the blank is in order. Referring to figure 65, cut along lines *B–X* and *A–X* with a hacksaw to remove that part of the blank. With the blank held flat, cut along lines *C–F* and *D–H almost* to the bottom of the bored portion. Now, with the blank held edgewise in the vise, cut from line *B–G* up to *C–F parallel* to the face of the blank to remove the piece *BCFG*. Do the same for the metal bounded by *DHI*. Remember, don't go all of the way to the bottom of the bored portion. With an 8-inch second cut mill file, file the flat area perfectly flush with the bottom of the bored portion. You

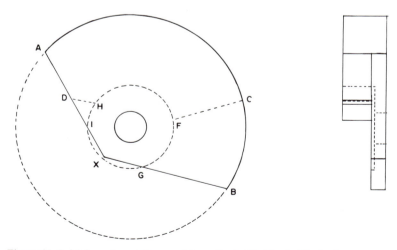

Figure 65. Initial rough metal removal from the bridle blank. The hacksaw comes into its glory here.

should now be able to put the tumbler in place on the plate and seat the bridle blank over it. The tumbler should now have a certain amount of rotary movement.

With the tumbler and bridle in place on the lock plate (the bridle should be positioned so it's in the same relative position to the plate top as on the drawing), clamp the bridle to the plate with a set of toolmakers' clamps. Check the tumbler for ease and smoothness of rotation. If it binds, either it was misaligned when clamped, or the filing of the bridle was incomplete. When the situation has been corrected, proceed with the next step. Remove everything from the plate. Using a cotton swab, apply a film of liquid soldering flux to that portion of the bridle that will be in contact with the lock plate. Do the same to the lock plate where the bridle will make contact. Do *not* spread the flux all around because there is a danger the solder could spread to the tumbler. Assemble the parts and clamp as before. Ensure that the tumbler can move freely and smoothly. Take a piece of plain wire solder (no flux core) and pound it flat and thin for about an inch. This will help it melt faster by concentrating the heat and permit it to be brought in contact with the parts to be soldered more accurately. Using a propane torch, apply heat to the side of the plate opposite that on which the tumbler assembly is mounted and directly under where the soldering will be done. Hold the solder against the metal at the juncture of the plate and the bridle. As soon as the solder melts, you'll see it seep in between the bridle and the plate. Remove the torch, and let the whole mess cool off. When it has cooled, remove the clamp and see whether the tumbler still moves freely and smoothly. If it does, good. If it doesn't, repeat the whole procedure until it does.

We're now ready to drill and tap the bridle screw holes and the sear pivot screw hole. For this operation, if you have a drill press, or access to one, you're in luck. If you have neither and you are using an electric hand drill, have someone with good eyes guide you to ensure that you are drilling square with the work. The holes will be drilled for a 6-40 screw. The finer thread is necessary in order to ensure the maximum number of threads in the thin lock plate. For the 6-40, a No. 33 drill is the size to use. With the tumbler-bridle assembly down, drill all three holes clear through the lock plate and the bridle. This includes the sear pivot screw hole. With the bridle still soldered to the plate, tap the holes from the outside of the plate, clear through the bridle. This includes the sear pivot screw hole. Although the holes in the bridle will be later enlarged with a body drill to let the screw through, the tapping is done in this manner to ensure that the tap goes in straight. If only the thin plate were tapped, the tap could go in at an angle. A deeper hold will correct any tendency to cant the tap. Use plenty of tapping fluid. Once the holes are tapped, unsolder the bridle from the screw plate. Clean up the solder from both the plate and the bridle with 220-grit wet-dry. The next step is to enlarge the holes in the bridle with a body drill. A No. 27 drill with a diameter of 0.144 inch is the recommended size given in various handbooks. Since the major diameter of a No. 6 screw is 0.138 inches, and we want a close fit, first try a $\frac{9}{64}$ drill. If the screws can be tightened down and alignment maintained, stay with this. If not, go with the No. 27 drill. The enlarged holes are now counterbored to accept a No. 6 fillister head screw. Don't counterbore the sear pivot screw hole any deeper than $\frac{1}{32}$ inch.

Assuming that everything in the preceding paragraphs was done properly, we now have a lock plate, tumbler, and bridle in perfect alignment. Further operations on the bridle will be performed to permit the full range of the tumbler swing, reducing the body bulk to accommodate to the lock plate and cosmetics. Lay out a circle of radius D plus 0.550 inch. Locate the tumbler pivot hole, the sear pivot screw hole, and the two holes anchoring the bridle to the lock plate (figure 66). Now, referring to figure 66A (don't let the apparent clutter throw you) and using the center of the three holes in the bridle, draw circles $\frac{1}{4}$ inch in diameter concentric with the screw holes and screw head counterbore. A $\frac{1}{4}$-inch diameter was almost arbitrarily chosen, since the final exterior shape around the hole will have sufficient metal around the screwhead counterbore, but still permit maximum metal removal. The circle around the tumbler pivot hole used as a guide in shaping the bridle is $\frac{5}{16}$ inch in diameter. This will permit $\frac{1}{32}$-inch addition to the bearing surface of the tumbler in the area where the metal is removed on the bridle. Draw lines A, B, C, D, E, and F tangent to the circles at points indicated by numbers 1 through 8. Set the compass to one and a half times the distance between tangents of the circles; i.e., one and a half times the distance between points 1 and 2, then between points 3 and 4, and so on. With this relationship in mind, strike arcs $1'$ and $2'$. Using their intersection as center, connect points 1 and 2. Continue this procedure for points 3-4, 5-6, and 7-8.

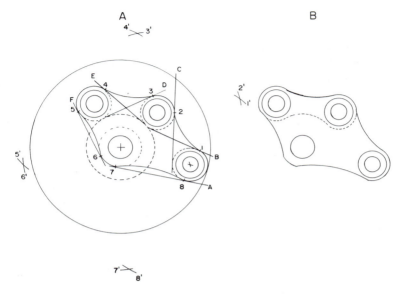

Figure 66. Layout for the final bridle shape.

When complete, the bridle without the lines, number, and letter adornment should look like figure 66B.

The completed drawing is now cut out with an X-acto knife, as were the previous templates. Carefully punch out the screw holes and the tumbler pivot hole, and paint the template with bright red nail polish. It will be necessary to align accurately the template with the rough bridle when gluing it on. This can be easily done by inserting the shanks of twist drills of the same diameter as the holes in the bridle through those holes. The holes punched in the template are then passed over the protruding drill shanks, and the gluing is completed with perfect alignment.

The bulk of the metal to be removed can be cut away with a hacksaw in a manner similar to that used when prepping the raw blank to be soldered to the lock plate. Be careful not to remove too much metal. Keep your cuts about 1/16 inch from the template. When the cutting is completed, further rough shaping can be done with the bench grinder. Once again, don't take off too much metal. The bridle is brought to its final shape and dimensions with the file. An 8-inch half-round bastard, 8-inch No. 0 pillar, and a 6-inch No. 0 three square should be enough to finish the job. The finished bridle should look like figure 66*B*. Note the radii on the underside of the bridle. They should be a continuation of the outside radius, merging with what remains of the original boring of the bridle blank.

COMPLETION OF SEAR

The major work in designing the sear was done in chapter 14, the nose, its curvature, and the location of the pivot hole. It is now necessary to give shape and dimensions to the remainder of the body and the arm. The position of the arm is now the critical factor in the design completion, since this is the part of the sear that will engage the trigger. As a rough rule of thumb, the pivot hole is twice as far from the arm as from the end of the nose. However, a more accurate method of determining its position is to measure the distance from the center of the top of the trigger portion that engages the sear to the rear end of the lock plate inletting, with the trigger assembly in place. The trigger is usually spring-loaded under a light pressure, causing it to bear against the sear. Because of this, it should be brought forward

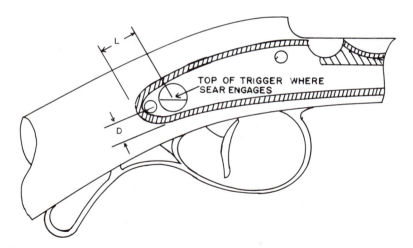

Figure 67. Layout to determine sear arm distance relative to lock plate end and bottom edge. Once again, this position is already established, and it's just a matter of transposing.

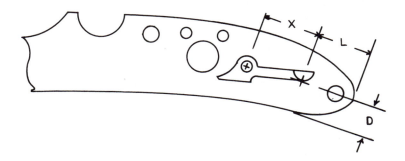

Figure 68. Transferring the positioning data from figure 67 to the actual lock plate. Use the sear pivot hole as a reference point.

almost to its farthest forward position for the next measurement. This measurement is from the middle, top of the trigger to the bottom of the lock plate inletting (figure 67). *L* is the distance to the rear of the lock plate inletting, and *D* is the distance to the bottom. These two measurements are now laid out on a drawing of your lock plate with the sear pivot screw hole accurately located (figure 68). The distance *X* is the distance between the sear pivot screw hole and the center of the trigger engagement. Utilizing the procedures of chapter 14, lay out the sear nose as in figure 61. It is now a simple matter to lay out the rest of the body based on the measurements *D* and *L*.

The ideal steel for the sear would be a piece of $^{13}/_{64}$- by $^{1}/_{2}$-inch flat ground stock, either oil-hardening or low carbon for case-hardening. This thickness would permit sufficient clearance between the lock plate and the bridle on the finished sear. Cut off a piece about 2 to $2^{1}/_{4}$ inches long. The reason for the long length is that the arm will be bent at a right angle to the body when the sear is filed out. The length of the arm will be measured from the lock plate to about $^{1}/_{16}$ inch beyond the thickness of the trigger top. On my gun, this is $^{7}/_{8}$ inch. Choose a spot on the steel blank to drill the pivot screw hole. Be sure you select a spot that will leave sufficient metal to permit construction of the sear. Drill the hole with a $^{9}/_{64}$-inch drill. Cut out the sear template, paint it with red nail polish, and accurately punch the pivot screw hole. Insert the shank of the drill through the hole to align the template, and glue the template to the metal. With a hacksaw and the bench grinder, remove the bulk of the metal almost to the template. This includes the body in back of the pivot screw hole for the entire length of the steel blank. Finish everything with a file right up to the template *except* the curvature on the nose that engages the tumbler. This area is filed *almost* to the template.

When the above operations have been completed, the nose curvature of the sear will be complete. This is really the most important part of the sear. The timing, trigger pull, and overall smooth functioning of the lock depend on how close the nose curvature rides against the tumbler, and how exactly the sear engages the tumbler notches. For this final fitting, all four components will be used: the lock plate, the tumbler, the bridle, and the sear in its present state of completion.

Cover the edges of the tumbler in the areas of the notches with a transfer agent such as Prussian blue (a thin coat is all that is necessary). Assemble the lock, including the semicompleted sear. With the tumbler in a position so that the sear is riding on the safety notch curvature, rock it back and forth, with pressure on the sear, so that the Prussian blue will transfer from the tumbler to the sear nose curvature. Remove the sear and examine it closely to determine where the tumbler made contact. The Prussian blue will mark the point or points. In all likelihood, you'll only have one spot. (A fit of twenty-five spots per square centimeter is considered "Wow!" An experienced toolmaker can do this. Don't feel disappointed if you don't; fewer will do nicely. Remember, you're working on an area of less than 0.050 of a square inch, or less than a third of a square centimeter.) Remove the sear and clamp it in a vise with soft jaws. Using a 6-inch No. 3 Swiss Pattern half-round file, lightly remove the high spots as indicated by the Prussian blue transfer. Concentrate on these spots only. Once this has been completed, cover the tumbler with Prussian blue again. Reassemble the parts, and effect the agent transfer again. Where spots appear, straight file them out. Continue the procedure until there is a good area of contact over the whole curvature of the nose. Be patient! This is not a ten-minute job even for a pro. When you are satisfied that sufficient contact is being made, draw file the curvature with a 5-inch No. 3 Swiss pattern three-square needle file to get a true surface. When this is done, wrap a piece of 220-grit silicon wet-dry around the half-round file and draw sand the curvature. Use a magnifying glass or loupe frequently to check the contact area.

The next area of contact fit is that of the sear-tumbler notch engagement. Recall the information from chapter 10 concerning the angles of contact of these two items. The Prussian blue will be of little use in this process because of the small areas of contact. Use a magnifying glass or a loupe. Assuming that the tumbler has been correctly filed, ensure that the sear makes complete contact with the tumbler full-cock notch. This includes both the angle of contact and the contact across the width of the sear and the tumbler. Use a 6-inch No. 3 pillar file on the sear. Be sure not to go beyond the template when completing this phase, or you might throw the lock timing off.

The last step in shaping the sear is to bend the arm at a right angle to the body and cut it to its proper length. In figure 68, X is the distance between the sear pivot center and the center of the arm. From the distance X, subtract one-half sear thickness. This is the actual distance from the pivot hole where the bend will take place. Lay out the distance and, with a three-square needle file, lightly file a line across the body. You will be marking the line where the bend will occur. The purpose of the filed line is that it will be clearly visible when the sear body is heated red-hot. Heat the body to red-hot with a propane torch, insert the after-part of the body in a vise exactly to the filed line, and make the bend. Use a hammer to ensure that the bend is complete and sharp. Work fast, because the small part will cool fast and you'll be pounding on cold steel with a strong possibility of break-

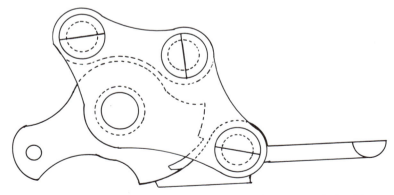

Figure 69. The tumbler, bridle, and sear assembled in proper relationship.

ing it. When the bend is completed, cut the arm to length. The end of the arm will protrude about ⅓₂ to ⅟₁₆ inch beyond the trigger when the lock is in place. Clean up the arm and body with an 8-inch No. 0 pillar file. Note that the bottom of the arm is radiused in order for it to ride smoothly over the trigger as it rocks. A square arm would have a tendency to catch on the trigger when it is in motion. The three parts assembled (tumbler, bridle, and sear) will look like figure 69.

16

Lock Completion

Now the whole lock will come together. The first job is to finish the lock plate. Note in figure 70*A* that the drawing of the plate appears "as is" up to this point with four additions: *A*, a block attached with a single screw just forward of the barrel cylinder recess; *B*, a new hole just to the right of the left-hand stock screw hole; *C*, a new hole just above and to the right of the sear pivot screw hole; and *D*, a new hole just above the rear stock screw hole. These new additions are to accommodate the mainspring and the sear spring. The block, *A*, properly called a bolster, provides the stop for the upper leaf of the mainspring; hole *B* is the pivot pin hole that provides the second point of support, at the V. Similarly, *C* is the screw hole that anchors the sear spring upper leaf, and *D* the pivot pin hole for the V. The location of all of these points is dependent on parts placement on the lock plate and the existing inletting on the stock. The upper leaf stop block, or bolster, on most front action locks is in the vicinity of the cylinder recess. On my gun, the position indicated in figure 70*A*, *A*, seems to be the most appropriate spot. From the space made available by the stock inletting, about ⅜ inch to the right of the center of the stock

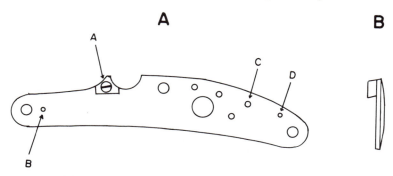

Figure 70. The completed lock plate with bolster attached.

screw hole seems to be the optimum location of the spring pivot pin hole. The sear spring hole locations were arrived at by similar guess work. Drill and tap the screw holes at A and C for a 6-40 thread. The pivot pinholes at B and C should be drilled for a $\frac{1}{16}$-inch hole. The block at A will not be attached and finished until all the remaining work is done on the plate.

Using undersized flathead wood screws, attach the plate to a piece of flat wood slightly thinner than the width of the plate, in a manner similar to the trigger guard work in chapter 11. The wood will provide a way of holding the work in a vise and permit full exposure of the plate so that it can be worked on. With a 10-inch mill bastard, draw file the length of the plate to give it a dome effect (figure 70*B* as viewed from the rear). Be careful not to file beyond the point where the plate is flush with the inletting. Finish the dome surface by "shoeshine" sanding with 120-grit silicon carbide or aluminum oxide paper or cloth. The final polish is given as described in chapter 12. After the plate has been domed and finish sanded, it will be heat-treated. A high carbon steel will be hardened and tempered in the conventional manner. To prevent the scale associated with heat treatment, the lock plate should be coated with a compound called PBS, available from Brownells, of Montezuma, Iowa. After the heat-treatment process, the plate will be frosty gray with no scale. Heat the plate to 1,450° to 1,550°F, and quench in the appropriate solution. The plate should be drawn (tempered) at 600° to 620°F. This is about spring temper. It is hard and tough enough to provide acceptable wear resistance and resistance to mechanical deformation, but not so hard as to be brittle. A file should just barely touch the finished plate.

The mainspring upper leaf retention block, or bolster, will be attached to the plate next. Select a piece of mild steel (1018 or 1020) about ½ inch square and ³⁄₁₆ inch thick. At about the center of the square, drill a No. 27 hole and counterbore it for a 6-40 fillister head screw. Thoroughly clean the area around *A*, figure 70*A*, with a 120-grit paper or cloth and a solvent. Do the same to the steel square. Attach the square to the lock plate with a 6-40 screw, so that its bottom is just about parallel with the bottom of the lock plate. Solder the two together, using the procedure previously described. This time, however, solder the screw in, too. Make sure solder gets into the screw hole of both the lock plate and the block. While the solder is still in the free-flowing state, tighten the screw securely.

Most solders melt at a temperature under 500°F. A common solder, 50-50, melts at just above 400°F. Since the tempering temperature of the lock plate was 600° to 620°F, soldering will have no effect on the temper, providing an excessive amount of heat was not inadvertently applied during the process.

When cool, file the block to conform to the lock plate outline. Clean up the solder on the block and lock plate with a file and 220-grit paper or cloth. The combination of solder and the 6-40 screw will provide sufficient rigidity and strength.

Next, cut a slot in the tumbler stirrup (swivel) arm to accommodate the stirrup, and drill a hole for the pivot pin. Figure 71*A* shows a side view of the tumbler in a rather awkward position. This is so the appropriate points can be projected to the edge view (figure 71*B*) relative to the completed slot *A*. The slot on my tumbler is ¹⁄₁₆ inch wide and 0.200 inch deep. This can vary for different tumblers. Make the initial cut with a hacksaw, with two blades side by side. (This will give a cut of about 0.050 inch wide.) Finish up the slot with a 4-inch joint round edge No. 2 cut and a 4-inch needle equaling file. The hole for the stirrup pivot pin is ¹⁄₁₆ inch in diameter. It is positioned in the center of the stirrup arm, about 0.075 inch to .080 inch from the end.

Figure 56 in chapter 12 has an isometric illustration of a typical stirrup. There is nothing sacred about either its shape or dimensions. This gadget serves as a free-moving link between the hammer and main spring. A flat oval would be just as effective as any other shape.

A   B

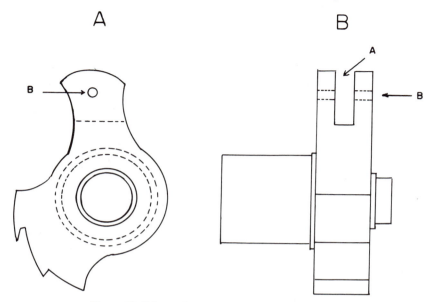

Figure 71. Stirrup slot and pivot hole in the tumbler.

The distance between the pivot hole and pivot pin should be such that the spring end is as close as possible to the tumbler stirrup arm, but the three, spring, stirrup, and tumbler, can move freely and without mutual interference. Like the other parts, the stirrup and the pins should be hardened.

SPRINGS

Few jobs present as much of a problem to the mechanic without a thermostatically controlled heat-treating oven as making a spring. The tempering temperature of a spring is critical. Too high a temperature will result in a wimpy, weak spring that will easily take a set in whatever direction it is bent. Too low a temperature will produce a spring so brittle that it is likely to break the first time it is bent. Somewhere in between the high and low extremes is the right range of temperatures. This range is narrow. Within it a spring can be tempered to produce a hard spring or a soft spring. A soft spring can be given a small permanent bend when it is bent beyond its spring range. A hard spring, on the other hand, would most likely break.

Tempering need not be an overwhelming obstacle to making a good spring. An accurate method of determining when the proper temperature has been reached was described in chapter 9. This is with the use of a heat-indicating lacquer with the trade name Tempilaq. Another excellent method of tempering is the lead bath. Pure lead melts at a temperature of 620°F. This is an ideal tempering temperature for springs. If you are a handloader who casts his own bullets, you probably already have the means to do this.

Of equal importance to the above is the proper selection of a steel. It's not good enough to hack a piece off an old automobile leaf spring and fashion your own. It may turn out usable or it may not. Some of the older springs were of a lower carbon content and would make a spring that is too weak for a gun. The best steel that is readily available for springs is carbon tool steel or drill rod. (Drill rod comes in round, square, and flat stock and is, in fact, tool steel.) A carbon content of 0.85 to 1 percent is most suitable for springs. I've found that any of these steels tempered in a lead bath (620°F) makes an excellent spring — not too hard, not too soft, but just right.

Proper leaf configuration and taper are extremely important if a spring is to perform well. A V spring must be tapered from its base at the V to its end, where the compression force is being applied if the stored power in the entire leaf is to be fully used. For you fly fishermen, picture a 7½-foot fly rod, 0.300 inches at the butt and 0.300 inches at the tip. This would be a straight tube, 7½ feet long, of graphite or glass, or a straight piece of bamboo of equal configuration. Now try casting your favorite trout fly with this contraption. You can't. The weight of the line and the fly simply won't load the rig sufficiently so that the latent power of the rod can cast them. Now configure the rod so that it is 0.300 inches at the butt, and with the proper combination of tapers, slims down to about 0.040 inches at the tip, and you can cast using the full power of the rod. The situation is similar with a flat spring.

Figure 72A illustrates a V spring with leaves of uniform thickness that sharply converge at the base. Assume that a compression force is applied to the open ends of both leaves. The major bending force is strongest at the base because that is the point of the longest moment arm for both leaves. As you move along the leaves toward the ends, where the force is applied, the length of the moment arm decreases. Consequently, the bending of the leaves decreases, until a point where

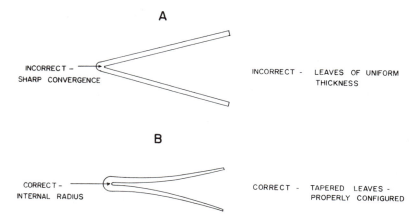

Figure 72. The right and wrong of **V** spring leaf tapers.

pound-inches moment cannot overcome the rigidity of the remainder of the leaves. As a result, only a portion of the spring leaves come into play for the final desired result. Figure 72*B* illustrates a situation where the leaves are tapered and properly configured so the compression pressure will be distributed over a progressive moment arm that will utilize all the potential of the leaf. Common sense and a good eye will tell you when you have the proper taper and configuration for a gun spring. In the above case, when the spring leaves are straight when completely compressed, you have a spring.

Mention was made of the problems caused by a sharp convergence of the spring at the **V**. It is a fact that, sooner or later, even the best tempered spring will break at a point where such a convergence occurs. This is a dangerous stress point. The convergence of the two leaves should terminate in a definite radius of about ¹⁄₃₂ to ³⁄₆₄ inch.

Figure 73 depicts the lock plate with the tumbler, bridle, and sear attached. Additionally, a swivel (stirrup) has been attached to the tumbler. *L1* and *L2* are the critical lengths of the main leaf (the lower) and the upper leaf, although the overall spring length will be longer than *L1*. The distance *L1* is measured from the main spring pivot hole to the swivel pivot pin. *L1* will vary as the spring is compressed and released. However, the swivel will compensate for this variance. *L2* is measured from the main spring pivot hole to the furthest point on the bolster. Similarly, *L3* and *L4* are the length dimensions of the sear spring. Unlike the mainspring, the upper leaf does not use a bolster as a stop. It is held by a screw (see figure 56, item 6). Also, on the mainspring the hook engages the swivel pivot. On the sear spring, the lower leaf merely presses down on the sear.

Select a piece of square oil-hardening ½ by ½ by (*L1* plus 1 inch). The additional inch in length is to provide sufficient material to work up the hook and the butt of the spring. Referring to figure 74, drill a ³/₆₄-inch hole ½ inch from one of the ends. This will be the termination radius of the two leaves. Using a hacksaw, trim the blank to the dimensions and shape down in figure 74. The little nub on the top of the rear end will become the spring pivot. With an 8-inch, No. 0 pillar file, file the nub approximately round. A roofing nail, or a similar nail with a large-diameter head will be soldered to the side opposite the nub, with the axis of the nail as perfectly in line with the axis of the nub as the eye can determine. The nail will be used to hold the spring blank in the homemade lathe so the nub can be turned to the spring pivot diameter. For solder, use one of the low-temperature, high-strength solders rather than the standard department store variety. The high-strength solders have a silver content, and some claim a tensile strength of 25,000 psi. Assuming that your lathe is rigid enough and that it turns at a low enough speed, you shouldn't encounter vibration because of the unbalanced workpiece. If you do, don't try to use it. Finish the job with a file.

Once the spring pivot has been completed, the recess of the hook that engages the swivel pivot pin will be drilled. Referring again to

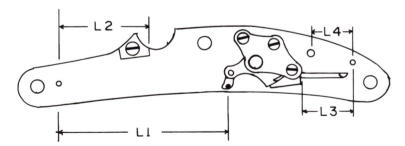

Figure 73. The lock plate with the tumbler, bridle, stirrup, and sear attached. Sufficient information is now available to arrive at both the mainspring and sear spring dimensions.

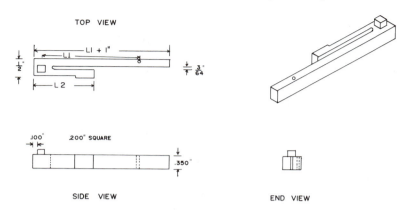

TOP VIEW

SIDE VIEW

END VIEW

Figure 74. A rough-cut blank for the mainspring. After drilling the hole separating the upper and lower leaves, remove the excess material with a hacksaw.

figure 74, at a distance $L1$ from the center of the spring pivot, drill a $\frac{1}{16}$-inch hole in the main leaf, favoring the outside of the leaf.

It will now be necessary to bend the rough blank into something that resembles the finished spring. This will permit working room for grinding and filing. Heat the blank to a blood red, and referring to figure 75, bend the leaves to the approximate shape shown in A. Allow the blank to cool slowly. Using the bench grinder for roughing and files for finishing, bring the blank to its final shape and dimensions. Once this point is reached, thoroughly inspect the spring to ensure that the leaves are smoothly and uniformly tapered and that no high spots, bumps, or sudden valleys are in evidence. When you are satisfied that the job has been properly done, polish the spring in its entirety. There can be no saw marks, file marks, or any other irregularity on the spring, as these will become major stress points resulting in the demise of all your efforts. The final result should resemble figures $75B$ and C.

The spring is now in its finished stage and ready for hardening and tempering. The scale associated with hardening is definitely not desired. Like the lock plate, it must be coated with a scale preventive. Once again, Brownells PBC is recommended. Heat the spring to 1,500°F and quench in oil. Two methods are readily available for tempering. The first method utilizes the heat-indicating lacquer Tempilac and the stovetop burner. Place a flat piece of metal about ¼ inch thick and 4 or 5 inches square, round, or whatever is available on top of the burner. Paint the spring with 600°F Tempilac and set it edgewise on the flat metal. Turn on the heat and when the Tempilac melts, wait about ten seconds and remove the spring. It's not necessary to quench it. The second method uses the lead pot. Pure lead melts at 620°F, an ideal tempering temperature for springs. Do not use your bullet-casting metal. If you don't have any lead, go down to your local garage and get some old lead wheel balancing weights. Chances are the guy will be happy to give you six or seven pounds if you're a regular customer. Melt the wheel weights in the pot, turn off the heat, and let it solidify. Then set the spring on the lead, on its edge. Turn on the heat again and when the lead melts, force the spring down into it with a metal rod. With the spring submerged in the lead, turn off the heat and let the lead solidify again. After about fifteen minutes, turn

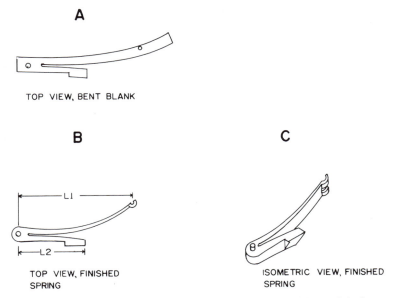

A

TOP VIEW, BENT BLANK

B

C

TOP VIEW, FINISHED SPRING

ISOMETRIC VIEW, FINISHED SPRING

Figure 75. Completing the spring. In *A* the spring is heated red-hot and the leaves are spread as indicated. It is then ground and filed to its final shape and dimensions.

on the heat, and when the lead melts, remove the spring and let it cool. The spring will have lead adhering to it. This can be removed with 120-grit paper or cloth.

The sear spring is made in the same manner as the main spring, so the procedures will not be repeated. Actually, it is a much easier spring to make.

THE HAMMER

The hammer can be as simple or as difficult to make as the gun-maker desires. All that is really required for it to function efficiently is that it be solidly attached to the tumbler, and that it strike the nipple or cap when released. Almost everything else is decorative.

Figure 76 indicates the reference points necessary to lay out the hammer. These are the center of the tumbler arbor hole, the top center of the nipple, and of course, the 45-degree angle that exists between a line drawn through the center of the arbor hole and touch-ing the center of the tip of the nipple. These three are sufficient to establish the center of the tumbler arbor hole and the location of the cup (the hole in the hammer nose that encloses the cap when the hammer is down) in the hammer nose. Figure 77*A* illustrates these

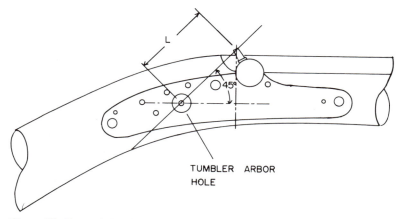

Figure 76. Determining hammer points and dimensions. Actually, a steel bar mounted on the tumbler arbor of sufficient length (*L*) to strike the nipple would work as a hammer. *L* is the one critical dimension. However, most people prefer a more ornate appendage.

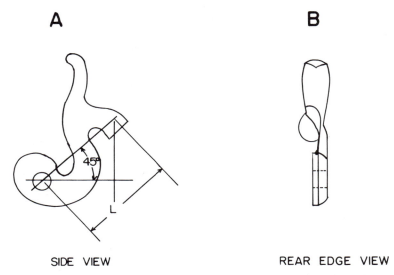

A   **B**

SIDE VIEW   REAR EDGE VIEW

Figure 77. A fleshed-out hammer of a basic design drawn around the dimension *L* and 45 degrees.

relationships. The distance L and 45 degrees are the position that the bottom of the cup should be when the tumbler is in the position shown in figure 61C. The overall shape of the hammer is up to the discretion of the maker. The one shown in figure 77A is a simple, functional shape. Some are so ornate they can be used as earrings. Select what you want, and go for it.

Lay out the points shown in figure 77A on a piece of cold roll ½ by 2 by 4 inches. Sketch in the desired shape around these points. Referring back to the procedures used in reducing the trigger guard pattern in chapter 11, do the same with the hammer outline. Punch, drill, and cut off the excess material. Rough shape the hammer with the bench grinder and bring it to its final shape and dimensions with files. The hole to accept the arbor should initially be drilled to ¼ inch diameter. File the hole into a ⁵/₁₆-inch square. The exact orientation of the square is not important, since the tumbler arbor will be filed square to accommodate the proper position of the hammer.

Figure 77B is the rear edge view of 77A. Note that the nose, head, and spur are offset to the left. This is because the nipple is always inward to the plane of the lock plate. The amount of offset can easily be determined by laying a straightedge against the lock plate and measuring the distance to the center of the nipple. A corresponding amount of metal is removed from the hammer body that faces the lock plate. The cup in the nose should be drilled to a depth equal to the length of the percussion cap, and about 0.010 inch greater in diameter.

When the hammer has been completely shaped and the arbor hole filed into a square, the next to the last step in the lock construction can take place. Remove the mainspring from the lock. Rotate the tumbler to the position shown in figure 61*C* and glue it in place using one of the modern super glues. (The bond can easily be broken with a little heat when required.) Paint the end of the tumbler arbor with layout fluid. Return the lock to the stock. Position the hammer so that the arbor hole is over the center of the tumbler arbor and the nose in a position where the cup would fully enclose the nipple. With a heavy-gauge needle, scribe the end of the tumbler arbor, using the square arbor hole in the hammer as a guide. Next, scribe a line around the circumference of the arbor just where it emerges from the lock plate. About 0.010 inch above this line is where the square on the arbor will end. The arbor is now filed square to accept the hammer.

The tumbler can now be hardened and, except for polishing the visible parts and blueing, the lock is complete.

Index